On Becoming Preschoolwise

Books in This Series

On Becoming Birthwise

On Becoming Babywise

On Becoming Babywise II

On Becoming Toddlerwise

On Becoming Preschoolwise

On Becoming Childwise

On Becoming Preteenwise

On Becoming Teenwise

ON BECOMING

PRESCHOOL WISE

Optimizing Educational Outcomes
What Preschoolers Need to Learn

GARY EZZO, M.A. AND
ROBERT BUCKNAM, M.D.

ON BECOMING PRESCHOOLWISE
Optimizing Educational Outcomes
What Preschoolers Need to Learn
Published by Parent-Wise Solutions, Inc.
(Parent-Wise Solutions is a division of the Charleston Publishing Group, Inc.)

© 2004 by Gary Ezzo and Robert Bucknam, M.D.
International Standard Book Number: 978-0-9714532-8-9

Printed in the United States of America

For information:
Parent-Wise Solutions, Inc.
2160 Cheswick Lane, Mt. Pleasant, SC 29466

09 10 11 – 9 8 7 6 5 4

Dedicated to:

Katelynn
An inquisitive mind,
a sweet spirit,
a gift,
a little girl

ACKNOWLEDGMENTS

Books are often a collaborative effort of many individuals whose gifts and talents help move a manuscript from scribbles to completion. This book is no exception. We desire to acknowledge and thank our educational consultant and long time friend, Robyn Vander Weide, for her insights and contribution to Chapters Six and Seven, *Getting Ready for Kindergarten—Now*, and *Developmental Placement—A Key to School Success*. Robyn describes the subject of preschool education with acuteness and clarity. We wish to thank Jenice Hoffman for her valuable advice and contribution to *Appendix A: Toys and Things*. In addition we wish to thank Carla Link, whose insights and assistance are found throughout in this book, including the rich source of good ideas found in Chapter Five, *Structuring Your Preschooler's Day*. Carla also provided accommodating thoughts in *Appendix A: Toys and Things* and joined our group of editors, Diane Wiggins and Tiana Wendelburg, to make this text better understood and readable. Last but not least, we note a special thanks to our friend and advisor, pediatric neurologist Dr. Rusty Turner, for flooding us with pertinent research papers during the review phase of this project.

CONTENTS

Introduction 9

Chapter One: Children Need to Play 13

Chapter Two: Factors of Learning 29

Chapter Three: The Voice Within 45

Chapter Four: The Choice Addiction 65

Chapter Five: Structuring Your Preschooler's Day 83

Chapter Six: Getting Ready for Kindergarten—Now 113

Chapter Seven: Developmental Placement—
               A Key to School Success 137

Chapter Eight: Laws of Correction for Preschoolers 153

Chapter Nine: Odds and Ends and Helpful Tools 173

Appendix A: Toys and Things 203

Appendix B: The Land of Good Reason 217

Subject Index 238

INTRODUCTION

Preschoolers are just plain fun. They know enough about life to enjoy it with enthusiasm and gusto, but not enough to survive very long without supervision. They are an independent lot, but would never want to be left home alone. They live on praise and encouragement, but a single stern look could bring them to tears. They can be shy and timid one moment, yet confidently insist "I can do it!" the next. They possess a ferocious appetite for play and order their lives according to the single principle that nothing is too difficult "for me." Play is their world and play is their tutor, taking them to the land of discovery that only ceases each night when they close their eyes in peaceful slumber.

Above all else, preschoolers are learners. Consider the amazing advancements in cognitive thought and physical adeptness achieved between ages three and five. Think about the myriad of activities that your preschooler can do right now. If a four-year-old wakes one morning in a home with no adult to assist him, and assuming he has a willingness to test his newly acquired power of self-rule, he could probably manage his morning activities. He would know where to look for his clothes and could manage to put on a pair of pants, pull on a shirt, and slip on some socks. While he may not be able to tie his shoes, he can manage Velcro. He could find his way to the kitchen and turn on the lights. If hungry, he would know where to look for bread, cereal, and peanut butter and crackers. It is more likely that a chocolate chip cookie, under such dire conditions, would be top priority on the list of food necessities! Pulling a chair to the counter, he could climb up to claim his favorite cup. While not masterfully, he could manage a butter knife and lift a quart of milk out of the refrigerator, although in the process of pouring it into his cup, he might

9

find equal amounts spilling onto the floor as in the cup. Or he might have already figured out that a juice box would suffice rather nicely. Junior might even venture next door to explain, in a four-year-old way, that Mommy was gone. Possibly he'd shake his weary head and explain, "Hey, it may have been last night's toilet paper incident that put the woman over the edge."

While the contextual setting above is very unlikely, and of course everyone realizes that a three- or four-year-old cannot maintain himself very long without adult supervision, it is a fact that preschoolers have gained some elementary skills basic to their survival that were not present just twelve months earlier. As he moves through the next twenty-four months, he enters a learning phase unlike anything yet experienced.

Through learning from his home relationships, the preschooler comes to know trust, love, comfort, and security in a much more personal way then before. Through learning from friends, he is able to measure himself against a world of peers. Through learning in life, he acquires competency in play, thought, work, and deed. Through learning of unconditional love, a child establishes his own unique selfhood. This growth period between ages three and five years is all about learning, and *On Becoming Preschoolwise* is all about helping parents create the right opportunities and best environment in which their preschooler can learn.

Our casual and professional observations of three- and four-year-old children draw us to three points of interest. First, as mentioned above, there is the matter of the developing imagination. At three years of age, make-believe and other imaginative activities begin to occupy an important place in the child's mental world. Imagination for the preschooler will do what curiosity for the toddler could not. It will carry your child beyond the boundaries of time and space. It can take him to places he has never been before. He can move mountains with his imagination and test his own feelings without fear of reprisal. Through the imaginative process, a child gives life to inanimate objects, while assuming a controlling role as chief operator of his own play.

Second, the emergence of the developing conscience opens the child to a world of moral awareness. While the study of the human conscience in preschoolers is less popular than the study of neural wiring or brain plasticity, it is a more important subject matter because the destiny of a child's life is shaped by it. There are some hard facts about the developing conscience that every parent needs to know, starting with the single truth that parents are the primary architects of the family conscience and that of each child. The home environment is the primary classroom, and parents are the first teachers, shaping beliefs and behaviors of right and wrong, good and evil.

The third point of interest is the preparatory phase of getting a preschooler ready for school. Longtime friend of the Ezzos and chief architect of their philosophy of education, Robyn Vander Weide, brings her many years of experience and insights as a professional educator, teacher, elementary school principal, and author to bear in Chapter Six, *Getting Ready for Kindergarten—Now*, and Chapter Seven, *Developmental Placement—A Key to School Success*. All the basics of school readiness are there for you.

And what about the daily grind? In Chapter Five, *Structuring Your Preschooler's Day*, Carla Link offers a workable plan and strategy that creates the intellectual ambience necessary to facilitate our three points of interest above. The most effective way to provide continual supervision for a preschooler and at the same time consistently provide a plethora of opportunities for learning is by structuring your child's day. The nuts and bolts and how-tos are clearly explained in Chapter Five.

We, of course, offer some guidelines for preschool correction and comment on topics pertinent to this age group—from understanding childhood fears to teaching manners and mealtime etiquette; from using positive speech to quieting the wiggles of an active preschooler.

On the technical side of this book, it is our custom to use the masculine references of "he," "his," and "him" in most cases. The principles of this book will of course work just as well with raising daughters. Further, we do not claim or insist that this is all the information you will need to raise a preschooler or prepare your son or daughter for school. It would take volumes more knowledge than we possess. Therefore, parents guided by their own convictions have the ultimate responsibility to research parenting philosophies available today and make an informed decision as to what is best for the family. Thank you for letting us share in your unique adventure of preschool parenting.

Gary Ezzo, M.A.
Robert Bucknam, M.D.

Chapter One

Children Need to Play

a little voice down the hall engages in a one-way conversation. "Now girls, look at Mommy's face and pay attention. We're going to the store and the two of you need to obey Mommy with a happy heart," says three-year-old Ashley to her favorite dolls. Seldom do we stop and think about the importance of imaginative play. Yet in the life of your child, it is a natural thing. In fact, various forms of play are one of the strongest indicators of healthy emotional growth and a significant component of a child's orderly development. Play is not simply a time when a child amuses him or herself. With all the pressure these days to educate young children early (even starting *in utero*), parents can take heart. One of the most active forms of learning is play.

In *On Becoming Toddlerwise*, we introduced our readers to the learning mechanism of curiosity and the role it plays in a toddler's learning ability. There we defined curiosity as a *natural* stimulus, a child's birthright—a survival mechanism. It is the key that unlocks the treasures of knowledge and opens a world of discovery for young children. Curiosity serves the child as a necessary precursor to the advanced skills of logic and reason.

While curiosity draws a child to an object, a second force holds him there. That force is *attention*. Attention is what holds a child in the moment of exploration, whether it is ten seconds or ten minutes. Attention is the power of attraction. *Attraction* is the result of sensory nerves working together, holding a child's interest to an object. It could be the color of a magazine, the shiny new pen, the odd-shaped lamp, or the musical ring of your cell phone. Color, shine, shape, and sound—all are in need of investigation. *Curiosity*, *attention*, and *attraction* all lead to investigation, which brings to the young child the excitement of discovery and learning.

A few short months ago, your toddler was sitting on the rug eagerly engaged in playing with a toy. As a toddler he was not limited by rules and regulations, starting or ending points of formal play. He played with the object as long as he wished and/or until he became interested in something new. He often manipulated his toy with his hands, pushing and pulling, pounding and banging, even attempting to test and taste the surface with small bites. The developing brain was working, processing, reinforcing, and gaining usable sensations. This is all part of a toddler's learning mechanism. In the process of investigative play, your toddler derived as much enjoyment from the stimulation of his senses and motor capacities as he did from the toy itself.

But as your child approaches three years of age, an even more powerful force comes into being. This force, your child's *imagination*, will cause you to marvel at its limitless possibilities. This natural endowment is a function of play as much as it is a function of higher learning. Whether this is accomplished through imaginative friends or educational toys, (see Appendix A, *Toys and Things*), it is part of your child's world.

Play and Imagination

Behold the wonders of your child's imagination! Evan rushes to park his bike on the front walk, grabs the coiled rope hanging off the back, and dashes for the front door. "Fire! Hurry! Spray the flames!" he shouts breathlessly, aiming the rope's end at the porch. Then circling back to the garage for assistance, he reaches for a make-believe axe to chop open an invisible door. One slightly amused black Labrador lifting her head for a second, curiously looks on. She's seen similar antics a million times before.

At three years of age, make-believe and other imaginative activities begin to occupy an important place in the child's mental world. Imagination will do what curiosity cannot. It will carry a child beyond the boundaries of time and space. It can take him to places he has never been. He can move mountains with his imagination and test his own feelings without fear of reprisal. Through the imaginative process, a child gives life to inanimate objects, while assuming a controlling role as chief operator of his own play.

In *On Becoming Toddlerwise* we shared the story of two-year-old R. J. and the Tommy Train he received for his birthday. At this age, R. J. showed only curious interest in the Tommy Train box cars and engine. He touched the tracks, spun the wheels, and even tried to stack the cars. But he did not understand how to play with a train.

At three years of age, the train set came out again and curiosity gave way to R. J.'s developing imagination. Now a more dominant cognitive process began to rule R. J.'s thinking. Now he plays the role of engineer. His mind constructs mountainous terrains out of pillows, wobbly bridges from a shoe box, and special tunnels through the legs of a chair. Train sounds begin to accompany each circle of the track as the train became real in R. J.'s mind. Big changes took place in one year. The same will happen with your child.

There is more! Your child's imagination is facilitated by another significant facet of a child's life, and that is *play*. Sometimes your child's imagination can interfere with your reality. Perhaps you casually remove the stuffed brown monkey from the kitchen counter only to learn you've inadvertently cut short his heat therapy by the toaster. Now someone besides the monkey is decidedly unhappy. Other times, and this is the good stuff, your child's imagination enhances your reality. In other words, Mom should take advantage of the child's imagination to achieve some healthy goals. Like when the lumps of steamed broccoli become foot soldier's preparing to march off to war against the formidable flu germ enemy causing his cold. Get clever, make his imagination work for you.

Play, whether a child does it by himself, in a small group, or with Mom at the park, is one of the most underestimated and often misunderstood components of a preschooler's healthy developing cognitive world.

Play creates learning opportunities and experiences that uniquely connect a child to his world, which otherwise could not be obtained. Through play, a child is first introduced to problem solving techniques, development of moral and social skills, improved motor coordination, logic, reasoning, and strategy. Plus, play has educational value and provides therapeutic benefits. Play complements and reinforces gender identification and encourages appropriate risk-taking. Overall, play is the single most important means by which a child connects with his world and the people around him. Think of play as the hub on a wagon wheel. Moving from the center outward, spokes connect to the outer rim of life and learning. Play generates multiple activities that goes into shaping the child, reinforcing values and stimulating learning. Please take note of this in our wagon wheel diagram.

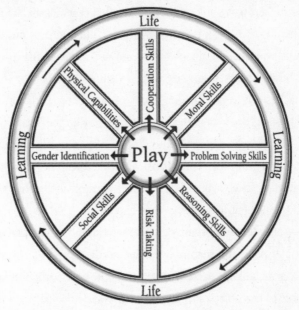

Everything about play accents a child's understanding of his world. From right and wrong to parental expectations, play reveals in a public way how a child thinks, reasons, and applies concepts learned the day before. Through his imaginative play, he mimics actions, traits, and social expectations by becoming another person and in this way he gains the experience of self-confidence necessary for proper socialization. By denying a child opportunity to play, a parent is in grave danger of collapsing the bridge connecting a preschooler's discovery, knowledge, and experience to learning.

The Benefits of Play

Play is your child's tutor. It goes far beyond simply encouraging learning activities. Through *attraction*, it becomes a means by which a child stretches himself beyond his present circumstances. He takes chances. When you think about it, play often contains an element of risk. There is some risk involved when a child ventures out on his first steps without the aid of Mom or Dad. There is risk involved when a child shares a new toy with a visiting friend or for the first time reaches out to pet the neighbor's puppy. There is risk involved when standing on a stage reciting a single line in the Thanksgiving play. He takes risks whenever the group's activities call for running, jumping, and bumping. There is risk associated with being picked on a team or not picked at all. In this sense, play motivates a child to step beyond the present to a new level of experience.

Play also has important educational value. During playtime a preschooler picks up, manipulates, and studies toys of all types. He learns shapes, colors, sizes, and textures and how parts of object fit the whole of the object. His mobility allows the development of life through the games he plays and the contact he makes with others. In time a preschooler learns to formulate plans, develop strategies, and exercise his assessment skills in problem solving because of play.

Developing socialization skills is one of the corollary affects of education. Through play, children learn that their personal gratification is often dependent on their cooperation with other children. Play teaches children about partnership, teamwork, and fair play. It is through play that a child's primitive understanding about "rules" is reinforced, because most games have rules. Interestingly, while the home environment may be more forgiving or patient with the bending of the game rules, it is quickly apparent to your child that his playmates are far less tolerant of a rule being violated. He quickly learns that he must "follow the rules" or be at the mercy of his peer group.

Play is also therapeutic both physically and emotionally. Physical play releases the pent-up energy stored during times of restriction. That is why recess time at the school yard is so noisy and fun-filled. The child is released to play with others. Physical play is a pressure valve allowing for the release of energy. In the preschool years, play must have some outside activity that has a physical dimension attached. Swinging, chasing after the dog, marching in Dumbo's imaginary parade, hide-and-seek, or any activity that can get their little heart pumping, growing legs moving, and developing minds stimulated provides therapeutic benefits.

Imaginative, emotional play is freeing to the preschooler. Such play allows a child to test his desires, fears, and hopes without the risk and hardships of judgments and boundaries associated with reality. He is able to think outside the boundaries of logic, reason, and reality. He is able to manage and direct ideas that only he understands and he does it in fragmented ways. He can take a big box and a blanket, make it become first Davy Crockett's fort, then a service station for his trucks, followed by a broadcast booth like the one he saw yesterday on television at the Macy's Thanksgiving Day parade. In any event, the child is in control of something he can control and should control. Children need to be able to control some things. Parents too often err in allowing these "things" to be Mom and Dad instead of the events of imaginative play.

A child's imagination leads to other forms of play. Preschoolers mimic. In our opening example, three-year-old Ashley recounted what she knew about going to the store with Mom and let her imagination direct her play toward her dolls. Obviously, she had an impression from her life that she transferred into her make-believe world. Thus both imitation and imagination work hand in hand.

The value of such play is worth noting. It not only stimulates a child's thinking, but also reflects what he is learning and how he is learning it. The next time you overhear your child's one-way conversation, listen carefully to the tone of voice used. For better or for worse, you might hear your own.

Another aspect of play is the element of *repetition*. Much more is taking place in a preschooler's play than what appears on the surface. Repetition gives the child the chance to consolidate skills needed to solve board games and puzzles, to stack blocks or connect Hot Wheels tracks. Even though your child appears to be doing the same thing over and over again, his activities are leading somewhere. For example, a four-year-old may have mastered elementary motor skills necessary for running and dodging a ball. Repetitious play advances him to the next level of skills called *anticipation*, where movements are predicated not as a response to the person throwing the ball, but to the anticipated throw itself. Here again, strategy, thinking, and reasoning skills merge to bring the reward of success. Success and accomplishment reinforce the cycles of learning.

Anticipation is not limited to the realm of physical movement but extends also to imaginative activity. To have expectations based on the belief of what will happen tomorrow, a child must be able to imagine. Imagining what will happen next, good or bad is part of the thinking exercise of our humanity. Parents give little consideration to the fact that if a child is in any way deprived of imaginative emotional play, either through discouragement or the lack of freedom at self-play, he will equally be deprived of what it is to know *hope*. For hope itself is not only a measure of the imagination transcending time and space, but of our very humanity. It all comes back to the importance of play.

Play also contains the element of construction. Man by nature is a builder. The Jewish Old Testament gives an account of a man named Nimrod called "the builder of cities" (Genesis 10:6–12). In fact, he built eight mighty cities by which he established his kingdom. One component of play common among children worldwide is the *construction* component. Children are builders and their efforts reflect the knowledge of our day. With their amazing imaginations, they construct buildings, boats, spaceships, mountains, overpasses, and tunnels. They use blocks, sticks, paper, and grass. They erect tall buildings out of discarded oatmeal boxes and bridges out of spare Lincoln Logs. Complete with sound effects, little boys move massive amounts of soil with their powerful diesel trucks, which may be nothing more than a thick piece of tree bark. Little girls also use construction in their play, but tend to make finer and more delicate objects such as doll clothes and paper dolls. They set up beautiful tea parties and arrange their neat little house with a few empty cardboard boxes, a folding chair, and a spare blanket. They love Grandma's old dresses and play endless hours as a beautiful princess or fancily dressed ladies right out of old Victorian neighborhoods.

It is through the medium of play that a child first develops his sense of fairness and cooperation and it is in play that moral strengths and weaknesses show up. How your child moves the board game pieces, scores his game, follows the rules, and shares with others reflects his developing moral identity. The child that sulks because he didn't get his own way or bullies, manipulates, or quits a game because he is not winning reveals much about a child's underdeveloped sense of fairness, sharing, cooperation, and justice. Play not only reveals moral strengths and weakness, but in the right or wrong environments, it can also encourage both.

But such moral attitudes, healthy and not so healthy, develop early and are continually reinforced by moral lessons taught throughout the day. Lessons in right and wrong and consideration for others, drives a child's social experience. Children do not like bullies and quitters, but they enjoy children who know how to play by the rules and love to share. Your child's moral sense creates either a positive, rewarding, and affirming response from other children or rejection. Most socialized play will always have a moral component. How well prepared is your child?

Play Has Limits

Does play have limits? Yes, several. Play has developmental, emotional, intellectual, and moral limits.

Play Has Developmental Limits

The technical word among clinicians for this type of limitation is *maturation*. Before certain types of play can be attempted, a child must demonstrate a level of maturity that includes the readiness of the mind and necessary motor skills to participate. If a child lacks basic eye-hand coordination, he is not ready for T-ball anymore than he is ready for an international Ping-Pong competition. But there is more to consider. Significant yet often elusive complements of physical readiness are the mental activities associated with play. These include a child's level of interest, his willingness to take chances, his self-confidence in play, his ability to overcome fearful anticipation of play, and the ability to handle defeat or victory that comes from play.

Also, the personal satisfaction derived from being able to do something well is an important influence on a child's development of "self." This was not a concern for your two-year-old, but it will be a concern for your four-year-old. If a child is rushed into any type of physical play that leaves him continually on the short end of victory because of the lack of readiness skills, he tends to back away from other good avenues of play that can lead him to competency in other areas of his life. When a child begins to shun games that test his skills because of a pattern of failure, he tends to form defensive strategies that carry into other fields of endeavor including school, friendships, and his own sense of self-worth. A preschooler who holds dearly to the belief that "I can't" because of repeated failures often translates this belief later in life to "I won't even try because I will fail." Be careful not to push your child prematurely into organized play activities prior to his readiness.

Play Has Emotional Limits

"My four-year-old falls apart if he doesn't win!" This statement usually signals that a child is playing a game beyond his emotional readiness. Such a condition is observed by this writer in casual observations of children, as well as experienced in his own home. Lesson learned? Do not push your children into games or types of play for which they are not emotionally ready.

Some games are too emotionally challenging for preschoolers. Your four-year-old should not be playing the marble-dice board game Aggravation (by Milton Bradly/Hasbro). The repetitive range of emotions experienced from excitement and anticipation of victory to a sudden loss of all your marbles (literally and figuratively) and imminent defeat are far too many emotional ups and downs for a preschooler to handle. We are not saying that your child should avoid games that challenge his emotions and test his limits, but rather to avoid games that are developmentally beyond his emotional limitations. If your child is routinely falling apart emotionally, the games he is playing are beyond his age-readiness. Going to bed with tears and a sense of defeat does not make for sweet dreams for your little darling.

Play Has Intellectual Limits

Because of differences in cognitive skill levels and childhood interests, preschoolers need to participate in types of play that fit their intellectual needs and abilities and can challenge their thinking without crushing their spirits. Pushing a child into a game before he is intellectually ready does not serve the child well. No matter how insistent your four-year-old might be, or how well he can "wheel and deal" with you, do not entertain the idea that he is ready for a game of Monopoly (Parker Brothers, 1935). He is simply not ready for the type of competition, the skill level, or the logic of buying and selling Pennsylvania Avenue property. Nor is he able to comprehend underlying meanings or sustain his own interest through the length of time is takes to finish the game. This will only lead to unnecessary four-year-old frustration.

Play Has Moral Limits

Children from the earliest days of memory face the impact of moral decisions and obligations made on their behalf and by themselves. From the time they were able to first understand language, they were reminded what is good, bad, approved, or naughty. The idea of what they are obligated to do or not do, how to behave or not behave, is fairly imbedded in daily thought and expected conduct. Therefore, any type of play that undermines or is antagonistic to your family's moral values should be avoided. Any type of play that weakens your preschoolers developing conscience undermines the fullness of his public character. Any type of play that interferes with basic respect for parents, property, and other people must be discouraged.

When you compromise the moral aspect of play, all sorts of bad things can happen to your preschooler's mental world, from poor self-esteem to poor play habits. This in time leads to weakened friendships and shunning from other kids. On and on the downward spiral goes when lines of moral play including fairness, sharing, and following the rules are crossed. The best prevention that parents can provide when it comes to play is stressing to their children that it must be "play by the rules" or "don't play at all."

Play Has Gender Limits

Every grandma knows that if you put a toy car, ball, stick, doll, blanket, and dishes in a room, little boys immediately gravitate toward the car, ball, and stick while little girls drift to the doll, blanket, and dishes. It really doesn't matter where a child is from, whether it be a complex society likes ours or a simple tribal setting in the rain forest. Little boys have a trail of masculine adjectives that distinctly separate them from little girls. Social conditioning? There might be some, but not sufficient enough to alter male and female predispositions embedded in nature's endowment of gender. The fact is, male and female brains are wired differently. Yes, little boys love trucks and little girls love dolls.

We bring this up as encouragement and as a warning. When it

comes to play, parents should not attempt to gender-neutralize their little boys or girls, but rather appreciate the differences and work with each propensity. A delightful example of this was demonstrated by Dr. George Lazarus, an associate clinical professor of pediatrics at New York City's Columbia University College of Physicians and Surgeons. He recounted a mother sensitive to gender-neutrality who gave her daughter several toy trucks only to find her daughter later tucking them into bed.

Understanding gender difference helps parents make proper evaluations about their child's progress both in play and life. It helps avoid speculative evaluations. For example, when a mother says, "But his sister was talking at his age," she is making a comparison in language development. But research confirms that girls tend to have a verbal advantage over boys early on. They speak sooner and more comprehensively by three years of age than their male counterparts who arrive at the same level of competency around age four and a half years.

Yet, boys have other strengths including aptitudes for math skills and completing calculations in their heads sooner then girls. Even the construction of their building blocks demonstrates gender predispositions, or lack of, toward engineering tendencies. Boys are also wired for action. That might be one reason they are always on the go, while their sisters are content to sit and play with their dolls or be entertained in a single location. This is why play is so very different for each.

Finally, notice how little boys play together compared to how little girls play. Girls are more relational and will work together to accomplish a common goal. Boys however, are far more likely to try and do things "on their own." Of course, any wife understands this truth. Just think through the times you may have offered directions to your husband only to hear, "I know where I'm going," as you're headed again for a wrong turn.

Summary

It is almost startling to realize just how important play is to a child's emotional, moral, and social development. Play is not simply an activity that a child wants to absorb himself in, but a necessary framework of understanding his world. As we have seen previously, play involves many facets and connects children to life in many ways.

But this too can be taken to an extreme with the old adage, "if a little is good, more must be better." Play is not an isolated experience in a child's life, but only one significant component surrounded by other aspects of education. Not all education comes in the form of play. A child will learn from playing with a toy, but more importantly he must develop specific skills that he can only gain at the hands of Mom and Dad. Sitting, focusing, and concentrating skills are not play, but they are necessary skills for life. Following instructions and being kind, fair, and honest will be used in play, but are not necessarily learned there. The learning process of these skills starts with Mom and Dad's acute awareness that a three-year-old heart is in need of training to think about the feelings of others first.

Chapter Two

Factors of Learning

ittle Stephanie waits patiently while her preschool teacher hands out the animal crackers. With camel, sheep, and monkey cookies placed before her, Stephanie looks up and with a gentle touch of her fingers to her lips she signs the words *thank you*. No one is surprised, then, when Stephanie, after carefully discarding her napkin, is among the first to respond when the teacher calls the class to reading time. While others in her group may be stimulated at home with flash cards and Spanish tapes, Stephanie's parents, along with many others in this new generation of Moms and Dads, have chosen to equally emphasize another component of development that includes: virtues, values, and Stephanie's heart.

This approach stands alone among the plethora of contemporary child-rearing theories vying for attention today. Here, for the benefit of those new to the *On Becoming* series, is a review of what we believe and why we believe it.

Just How Smart Is Your Preschooler?

Go ahead and boast just a little, because cognitively, your preschooler is truly amazing. Learning continuously occurs through interaction with her environment. Yet, a preschooler's interpretation of these new experiences flourishes only within the context of knowledge already gained and understood. This is a critical point. Learning for all of us is progressive, built piece upon piece. Your little person is no different. She will only gain *understanding* when new information has meaning in relationship to previous experiences. Pushing a jack-in-the-box off the edge of the counter may cause it to burst open. Then again, it may not. Either way, the true joy of the toy is missed. Only after careful study, demonstration, and moments spent fiddling with the box does the preschooler appreciate the very definite cause and effect of this toy. Another push off the counter is merely hit and miss.

Routine and orderly transition at each stage of a preschooler's development aid the marriage between new information and a preschooler's understanding. Learning is positively impacted by order and routine and negatively impacted by random chaos. For a preschooler, rummaging through an cabinet, discarding its contents, bursting forth to overturn counter stools, and then running to the fridge for magnet rearranging is most certainly chaos of the random kind. While sorting through new information in an orderly fashion allows a child to accurately learn cause and effect, an environment where the child is left to roam at large offers random reactions. Here the child has nothing sensible to assimilate.

The child who can associate right meanings with new experiences is far more advanced in his or her understanding than the child who must associate a new meaning with an old situation that stands in need of correction. The latter, sadly, is a common legacy of laissez-faire (permissive) parenting. Since learning comes in progressive stages, training should take place progressively as well. For this reason, parents need to provide their child with a learning environment that matches *information* with *understanding*. This is more simple than you might think and far more beautiful than a kitchen covered with pots, pans, and toys strewn everywhere. There are many factors that influence learning, both positively and negatively. The child's temperament, the presence or absence of siblings, parental resolve, the purpose for training, the method of instruction, and reinforcement are some of the more obvious ones. Generally speaking, you will spend all of your parenting years in three arenas of knowledge.

These three arenas of knowledge are:

- Instructing your children in matters of life skills (health and safety)
- Intellect
- Morality

Let's take a look at each one.

Skills

Not all behavior is moral in nature. Some actions are morally neutral—such as those related to basic skills. One of the most important and most rapid areas of development during the early years of a child's life is the development of motor skills. Learning to use a spoon, walk, swim, tie a shoelace, ride a bike, kick a ball, and climb a rope are amoral (neither moral nor immoral), stage-acquired activities. They are skills associated to a large extent with the child's environment, opportunities to learn, and his motivation to do so. From the helpless state of infancy, the development of skills like the ones mentioned above begins and moves forward. Most children learn these feats in progressive stages. For example, when a toddler throws a ball, he uses his entire body. As coordination develops, your preschooler will begin to throw the ball using only his arm.

Skills, talents, and giftedness are not the same. Skills, such as learning to walk, coloring within the lines, riding a bike, learning to swim, and throwing a ball, are basic to all human beings. Natural talents differ from skills in that they are discriminatory. Some people may have a particular talent that others do not. All of us have talents, but not necessarily the same talents. Giftedness is a talent magnified. Many musicians are naturally talented, but Mozart was gifted.

Intellect

Intellectual learning is the accumulation of data and the ability to apply logic, or reasoning skill, to given situations. Academic learning, much like physical development, moves from general to specific and is progressive. We teach our children the alphabet so they can learn to put letters together to form words and then read those words. They first learn to count—1, 2, 3, 4, 5—but it will be a while before they realize that those numbers also can represent 12,345. Children first learn about trees and then begin to distinguish, for example, pine trees from oak trees. Eventually, they will also learn to identify the different varieties of pine trees.

Moral Training and Collateral Value

While academic training is important, it is greatly supported and enhanced with moral life skills. The nature of moral training and the components of character formation create the infrastructure of logic and reason, which is borrowed by the intellect. In time, this advances the child's overall cognitive skills. By that we mean moral training has accompanying corollary value that academic training does not. Because moral training is a highly integrative process (moral thought + moral action = doing the right thing), the integration pathways of learning in general are multiplied and thus borrowed by the academic side of the preschoolers organizing brain. This is why we are strong advocates of parenting the *"whole child."* This concept, while developed more fully in the next book in this series, *On Becoming Childwise*, has earned a place here for preschool parents.

The Whole Child

Happily, within educational circles today, there exists a healthy movement away from single-focus parenting. A growing consensus of parents appears to be in favor of parenting the *whole child*, with its corollary benefits.

This term implies a child-rearing approach that considers the natural capacities of children as the primary targets of parenting. It is the counterweight to, on one hand the unbalanced, child-centered, permissive approach that elevates a child's happiness over his moral sensibility. On the other hand, it strikes a counterbalance to the strictness of authoritarian parenting. This approach regulates behavior often at the expense of a child's developing emotions.

The essence of the whole child can be measured and understood by the natural capacities of children.

There are four general capacities:

- Children have physical capacities. The duty of parents is to nurture and provide for their children's physical growth and well-being. Parents feed, clothe, and shelter their children and encourage the development of the natural skills and talents necessary for life.
- Children have intellectual capacities. The duty of parents is to stimulate their child's intellectual competency. Parents educate their children in basic skills, logic, and useful knowledge.
- Children have emotional capacities. The duty of parents is to nurture their child's emotional well-being. Parents help their children establish internal controls over both positive and negative emotions.
- Children have moral capacities. The duty of parents is to help their child internalize virtues that reflect the values of the family and society.

All four facets receive attention. None should be neglected, underdeveloped, or overemphasized. Why is that? Understand that for children, competence and character will go hand in hand. Think of these four areas described above as building blocks.

The Ezzo/Bucknam *whole child* approach assumes that one arrangement of the blocks is indeed better than all others. In fact, disagreement between parenting philosophies usually center on which building block is to be awarded priority in the construction of the whole child. The importance of moral education cannot be overstated. Not only should moral teaching be the priority of early training; we believe that moral training is absolutely essential for your child's optimal intellectual and emotional development, as well as his advancement of natural skills.

For most parents, moral training already takes center stage. They just don't realize the room they've given this building block. Think about it—what is in your preschooler's book and video collections? How many *Winnie the Pooh* or *Veggie Tales* videos does your child own? Preschoolers love these and retain the moral lessons learned. What about the storybooks you're reading to them? What truth is being imparted? Don't doubt it for a second—you spend many hours teaching virtues to your children.

How It Works

Moral training has a corollary impact on the other capacities. It gives children advanced modes of thought that are more easily transferred to both the intellect and emotions than through any other form of education. Moral training provides the objectivity needed for emotions to function freely without overpowering the child. As a result, you are much more likely to successfully parent the whole child. Moral training, done right, delivers the whole package: emotionally balanced, intellectually assertive, morally sensible children, raised to the applause of a grateful society.

For example, by the time your child is three years of age, he is ready to learn to interrupt your conversations courteously. Granted, initially he may not be overflowing with joy at the prospect of demonstrating politeness. Neither was he eager to pick up his toys once the novelty was gone. Nevermind the child's point of view. You teach the behavior for a greater triumph. Look carefully at how moral training in this area has a corollary impact on learning.

The Interrupt Courtesy

We've all been there. There are few disrespectful actions worse than having a conversation rudely interrupted by a demanding child jerking on Mom or Dad's arm, insisting on an immediate audience with total disregard for the context into which he is stepping. Usually a child doesn't know any better because he hasn't been taught any different.

There is a moral way to handle this. Teach your little one how to interrupt your conversation politely. This is a moral skill that shows preference to others. A simple technique eliminates this problem. When your child needs to interrupt you, teach him to place a hand on your side, shoulder, or arm and then wait the few moments it will take for you to acknowledge him. This process can be taught to a child as young as eighteen months old. These kids catch on quick.

From the child's perspective, the hand on your side silently means, "Mom, I realize you're talking with someone else, but when you get a moment, may I ask you something?" The child learns that you will indeed find a place in the conversation to politely say "Excuse me" to the person you are speaking to and give the appropriate attention to your child. It creates a win-win dynamic for you both. This gesture beautifully displays respect for you and for the one to whom you are speaking.

Also, when your child puts his hand on your side, take your hand and place it on his, gently squeezing it. This lets him know that you know he is there. Often the reason a child pulls on Mom and verbally interrupts her, insisting on attention, is because he is not sure she knows he is there. He is attempting to make his presence known. The little squeeze affirms to him your awareness of his presence.

Teaching your preschooler an appropriate way to interrupt a conversation is a gesture of honor and respect. You can use this tool when on the phone or talking to the child's sibling. Teach it as an act of courtesy.

Please note these resulting effects:

- The child learns to trust that the parent will meet his needs in an orderly way.
- It helps the child to grow in the virtues of patience.
- The child learns self-control.
- The child learns attention skills.
- He learns to think before acting.

Think about it. Order, patience, self-control, attention, thinking before acting—all are prerequisites to learning. These are habits of moral logic easily transferred to the academic and skill side of your preschooler's brain. Please note that the process doesn't work in reverse. Playing with blocks, putting puzzles together, and matching colors are important activities of learning for your preschooler. Yet such activities have value only to the extent that it is part of the learning process. They have no more collateral value as it relates to character training than brushing his teeth does to a preschooler. Learning to count from one to ten or picking colors from a chart does not make your preschooler kinder, more self-controlled, or easier to manage. Such education is important (we are dedicating an entire chapter to this), but its value is limited to the arena of knowledge, not behavior.

Immediate Gratification or Self-Control

Finally, we offer encouragement about self-control training. Generally speaking, achieving healthy learning patterns is the child's first step toward understanding. We know that a basic routine enhances the establishment of those patterns. When a child is at peace with his basic environment, his learning potential increases and learning disorders are minimized.

Timely gratification training leads to greater self-control in children, which then leads to longer attention spans and an advanced aptitude for academic and moral learning. The key term here is *self-control*. Self-control is a base virtue. That is, other virtues and life skills in an individual can't exist without it. Self-control influences kindness, gentleness, proper speech, the ability to control negative emotions, focusing skills, sitting skills, and many other behaviors. Each of these has a corollary impact on learning. When you train your child to a right moral response, you simultaneously train him in self-control.

Why is that true? Because self-control is not an academic discipline—it's a moral one. Sitting, focusing, and concentrating are also moral disciplines borrowed by the intellect to advance academic achievement. No training in moral self-control is ever isolated. The self-control needed to sit, think, and choose a better way to communicate is the same self-control that will safeguard a child through life. Such self-control is the product of moral training and not the result of memorizing flash cards or playing educational games. Consider for a moment the child next door, down the street, or in your child's play-group who lacks age-appropriate self-control. Take note of his emotions.

When emotions are strong and persistent, damaging effects multiply. The way a preschooler learns to express his emotions carries over to adulthood. The way he learns to respond emotionally will not only affect the quality of his behavior but will influence the judgments of other people and their attitudes toward him.

That is why waiting until a child is five years old is much too late to start working on the skills of sitting, focusing, and concentrating. These are moral developmental skills, not activities acquired with age. They are skills that depend on orderly structure. You are laying the foundations for future development. Healthy moral development pays dividends in many ways.

Can parents alter their child's intelligence quotient (IQ)? No. Can they maximize or limit it? Emphatically, yes! We maintain this perspective because we have consistently found that parents who rejected structure from birth, and did nothing to correct a lack of structure in the preschool years, had actually slowed and in many cases corrupted the process of moral and intellectual development. Do the premises we present represent theory or reality?

It was with great interest and pleasure that we read the cover story of *Time* magazine, "The E.Q. Factor."[1] The article spotlighted the work of Harvard University professor Daniel Goleman. In his book *Emotional Intelligence*, Dr. Goleman presents some very interesting findings. He states that children who gain the mastery of delayed gratification learn the virtue of self-control and hence have a much better life. Children trained in immediate gratification suffer and are left behind.

....
[1] See Nancy Gibbs, "The E.Q. Factor," *Time* (October 2, 1995), 60.

His study began with a marshmallow and involved a test developed by Dr. Walter Mischel of Columbia University. One at a time, children were brought to a room and offered a marshmallow. They were told they could eat the marshmallow "right now," or if they waited until the researcher got back from running an errand, he would give them a second marshmallow. But they had to wait and not eat the first one. After the test was completed, researchers followed these children as they grew up. This is what they found: By the time the children reached high school, the children's parents and teachers found that those who, as four-year-olds, had the fortitude to hold out for the second marshmallow generally grew up to be better adjusted and more popular, adventurous, confident, and dependable teenagers. The children who were raised with immediate gratification training, who could not wait for the greater benefits, were more likely to be lonely, easily frustrated, and stubborn. They buckled under stress and shied away from challenges. When comparing their scores on the Scholastic Aptitude Test, the kids who waited for the second marshmallow scored on average 206 points higher.

The article cited above offered Dr. Goleman's conclusion: "It seems that the ability to delay gratification is a master skill, a triumph of the reasoning brain over the impulsive one."

We spoke by phone with Dr. Walter Mischel of Columbia University to ascertain the length of time the children waited between marshmallows. He told us that the original study used a delayed gratification factor of fifteen minutes. We then repeated the test with twenty-five children, ages three, four, and five years, whose parents had used the principles in *On Becoming Babywise* when these children were infants. For our three-year-olds, we set the gratification factor at ten minutes. But we extended Dr. Mischel's time by five minutes for the four- and five-year-olds, making the children wait twenty minutes. This is what we found:

- Of the 5 three-year-olds tested, all waited for the second marshmallow.
- Of the 15 four-year-olds tested, all waited for the second marshmallow.
- Of the 5 five-year-olds tested, all waited for the second marshmallow.

Dr. Goleman's research focused on the result of delayed gratification, but not on the method of achievement. Yet obviously all the children we studied demonstrated a conscious choice for delayed gratification for the greater gain. Could something as basic as an infant feeding routine, healthy naps, continuous nighttime sleep, definite boundaries, and a healthy dose of *otherness* training be the channel for success? We believe so.

Boundaries, Emotions, and Self-Control

Every child enters life with the propensities for both pleasant and unpleasant emotions. Most parents realize this truth and consequently attempt to find ways to make childhood a happy time for their offspring. Parents recognize that a happy child is a pleasure to be with, easier to teach, and exhibits longer sustained periods of self-control and self-entertainment. But is happiness the highest driving force and the ultimate goal of parenting? We hope not!

One of the greatest mistakes parents make is an attempt to parent a child's emotions and not the child. Please note this distinction.

We are not saying a child's emotions are not important, but rather attempting to parent the single category of emotions is not the same thing as attempting to parent the *whole child*.

Every child will experience both pleasant and unpleasant emotions. Hopefully, your child will know much more of the first than the second. The experience of positive emotions, joy, happiness, affection, self-esteem, and the sense of discovery lead to feelings of security and confidence. This in turn helps the child face and properly react to the negative emotions of worry, jealousy, envy, fear, disappointment, anxiety, and frustration. But parenting with a philosophy that attempts to create only positive emotions while avoiding all negative emotions is both unwise and unhealthy.

The Happiness Quotient

For some mothers the ideal emotional state of any child is one wrapped in endless happiness. Such a pursuit is not only impossible but produces a predictable pathology in children that is not good. The child that is pampered or shielded from unpleasant experiences may have moments of temporary happiness, but he is ill-prepared to meet the disappointments, frustration, and other unpleasant experiences that will confront him just outside the front steps of his home, when his parents can no longer completely control his emotional environment.

Because happiness is viewed as the "highest value," all other "good" values—such as honesty, compassion, self-control, self-entertainment, obedience, submission, and patience—play only a subservient role in the life of the child. If conflict occurs between any of the subservient values and happiness, happiness must prevail. It is the trump value. Whenever you focus on a single value and elevate it above other "good" values, you move into extremism.[2] An extremist is not simply a person that holds a different point of view than you, but one who elevates a single good value above other equally good values and thus closes out the benefits the other values can bring into his life or the life of his child.

During a recent time of questions and answers, a mother posed her dilemma. Her four-year-old son continually took advantage of his two-and-a-half-year-old brother during playtime. The most common violation was his refusal to share with his younger brother and hoarding all the toys. The mother thought correction was the right thing to do, but every time the older sibling was removed the younger brother would cry. "What is better?" the mother asked. "Disciplining my four-year-old, even if that makes his younger brother sad, or ignoring the sharing problem and keeping both boys happy?"

Our evaluation of this situation brought us back to the principles of this chapter. This mom placed greater value on the younger son's emotions than on her older son's character faults in need of correction. She was willing to allow her older son to bully his sibling for no other reason than she feared her younger son would not be happy for a moment.

We're pleased to say that we were dealing with a very open and teachable mom who created for herself a clever reminder. She hung on her refrigerator door a small chalkboard. On it she wrote, "Parent the whole child, not the single category of emotions." That friendly reminder stayed there until the principle was second nature to her.

---

[2]For an expanded discussion related to the dangers of extremism, see Dennis Prager's essay, _Why People Become Extremists_. (_Think a Second Time_, Regan Books, 1995), 159-165.

As a result, today she has a four year-old who shared his things, and a happy two-and-a-half-year-old.

Summary

When you attempt to parent your child's feelings, you are forced to abandon other significant values necessary to raise well-adjusted children. Immediate gratification becomes dominant. Parenting a single emotion or a range of common emotions is a poor substitute for parenting the whole child—his heart, head, body, and emotional being.

We promise you this: If you parent the whole child and not random emotions, if you allow your beliefs and family goals to guide you, if you work on creating a trusting environment that includes a strong, loving, and vibrant marriage, you will produce the following:

The *Babywise*, *Toddlerwise*, and *Preschoolwise* child is generally socialized, cooperative, and friendly. As a rule, he is honest, dependable, faces life confidently, is self-reliant, and adjusts to new social situations. He is neither overly fearful nor anxious, nor does he experience emotional meltdowns when he does not always get his own way. He sleeps well, eats well, and plays well. He can entertain himself when need be and equally enjoys other children demonstrating the virtues of sharing, kindness, and empathy. He is loyal, emotionally stable, and cheerful. He accepts responsibilities and restraints. Obedience is willingness based on his trust in Mom and Dad. He cares for his property as well as for that of others and is well on his way to a life of empathy. As a rule and as a result, he is a happy child.

The rest of the book is dedicated to helping your child achieve the character traits just listed. It is not always easy, but it will always be worth it.

Chapter Three

The Voice Within

"Caleb, I found these two Matchbox cars near the couch," I said, handing our three-year-old guest the sleek, shiny, new red and white cars. "You must have missed them when you cleaned up the track you brought over." The little blond-headed boy turned over the cars placed in his hands. Widened eyes belied his intuitive comprehension of what it would mean to add these beauties to his collection. Yet he paused midway through that thought. Something seemingly stopped him cold; then he lifted his head, shaking it slowly back and forth. "No, these are not my cars. They belong here. Mrs. Ezzo keeps them for children who visit." Caleb reached out and placed them carefully back in my hand.

Let's look at the facts present in this scenario. Fact one: the cars did not belong to Caleb. Fact two: he knew it. Fact three: Caleb was the only one present who had all the facts. He could have easily taken the cars home with him. After all, Mr. Ezzo offered them to him. Incredibly, he did not. Here, moral sanctions were at work in a three-year-old heart. Sooner or later every child makes decisions based on what he believes to be right. Indeed, all children from age three years and up begin to acquire a functioning conscience, controlled by a developing system of beliefs, ideas, values, and virtues that internally decree what is right, wrong, good, or evil. This is what determines how one should respond to situations. In the case above, Caleb's conscience had arrived.

What occurred inside Caleb's heart can take place inside the heart of your preschooler. This special "something" acts as the silent voice stirring within the heart, monitoring conduct for moral accountability. Yes, even starting at three years of age. As Mom will not always be with her preschooler at all times, this "something" will be everywhere your preschooler goes—whether it be to visit Grandma, the playgroup, or at a family reunion, where all the kids merge into one noisy herd sighted in hourly intervals around the cooler full of drinks. This special something is known as the conscience.

While the study of the human conscience is less popular than the study of neural wiring or the complex workings of the brain, it is a more important subject to ponder. You see, the destiny of a child's life is shaped by his conscience. To be quite honest, as an educator and medical clinician, we are surprised by the absence of public teaching on this subject, especially when it comes to child training. We suppose conversation about the conscience could be politically incorrect. It is possible that guilt and shame, two components associated with the conscience, are now socially considered vices of the soul rather than reflectors of moral misconduct. If that is the case, guilt and shame are getting a bad rap.

There are some hard facts about the developing human conscience that every parent needs to know. It starts with the single fact that parents are the primary architects of the family conscience and of each child within the family. In the beginning, a child has no functioning conscience, no preset scale of values. Before he can behave morally, he must learn *general* concepts of right and wrong and then advance to *specific* concepts of right and wrong. The home environment is the primary classroom, and parents are the first teachers.

How one learns to get along with other human beings shapes his future as much as a good education or any acquired skill. The essence of community is bound by the reality of our collective conscience. A good conscience prevents calamities, afflictions, and miseries. What good health is to the body, a good conscience is to the soul. There is inward satisfaction of conscience when a good action is done, when virtue is practiced. The most natural beauty in the world is honesty and moral truth.

The Conscience—What It Is and How It Works

"Something's stinky here!" blared Erin, stepping off the elevator onto the full-time care floor at the nursing home. Heads turned, and since the messenger was barely more than two feet tall, smiles erupted. This time anyway. Yet between that moment and the next several inches, a moral truth regarding kind words needs to be planted in this preschooler's conscience.

The conscience is a moral faculty, a guiding voice from within, the faculty or principle by which we distinguish right from wrong. It's the voice that helps us control our thoughts and actions and monitor our words. In everyday life, one can find illustrations of a properly working conscience—from determining whether a Matchbox car belongs with your collection to returning the extra money that a clerk mistakenly gave you when making change for your purchase. And every day one can find illustrations of a not so well-trained conscience—lying about cheating or keeping money that is not yours.

To act against the conscience is to act against moral reason. The conscience raises its voice in protest whenever anything is thought of or done contrary to the values of the heart. As a mentor and a friend, it warns you that danger could be ahead while you are still thinking about how you are going act. When you have done something you know is wrong, it punishes you as a judge. Conscience is the voice of Self, which says yes or no when you are involved in a moral struggle. It is a call from within to act rightly or avoid wrong. And it flashes the warning to keep quiet when something's stinky.

The conscience, then, is the seat of moral testimony. It is that portion of our humanness that receives and reflects values that represent what the mind perceives as morally right and wrong, good and evil. Most importantly the conscience is not something you stir up in a child, rather something you shape in the child—carefully and with purpose.

In our preceding book, *On Becoming Toddlerwise*, we asked the question: "Where do parents focus most of their training energy?" For young children it falls into these four arenas:

- Health and safety
- Life skills
- Moral training
- Teaching submission to Mom and Dad's leadership

When referring to moral training, we are specifically addressing how parents influence the habits of the heart and train their children both in virtues of life and the governing values of the family.

The activity of moral training has a specific destination within the child. The final stop is a fully shaped, faithfully functioning conscience. Prior to three years of age, moral training centers on controlling outward behavior and pointing the child in the right direction morally speaking. That approach takes priority because prior to three years of age, a child's intellect has not reached sufficient maturity, nor is it advanced enough to understand how the virtue of "otherness" (putting others first) works. Nor is there sufficient moral self-control to consistently apply virtue. The *me, myself,* and *I* phase is still operative and continues to be so up through the age of three years.

However, around three years of age, your child's intellect is sufficiently developed to the extent that he is ready to receive the *why* of moral training. The *me, myself,* and *I* phase begins a metamorphosis from the dominate "me-ism" to the practical "we-ism." Emphatic feelings for others start to emerge and virtues begin to make sense. At three years of age, your child is ready to receive basic moral precepts upon which he will build a lifetime of values.

A Walk in the Park

Here's where it starts. It's springtime and two-year-old Becky is strolling with Mom through the formal gardens at the park. Beautifully arranged tulips in full bloom appear along the pathway ahead. Becky wanders over and reaches out for a tulip. Instantly envisioning the scenario of falling petals and a flowerless stem, Mom calls out, "No, Becky, don't touch the tulips." Becky pulls back her hand, restrained by Mom's instruction. Becky has already learned that disobeying Mom brings a consequence. That part is not new. She mimics right moral actions (she didn't pick the tulip) only because Mom made it happen and not for any altruistic reason on Becky's part. At two years of age, Becky has neither the moral or intellectual capacity to understand that if every child walking in the park picked the pretty flowers, there would soon be no flowers left for others to enjoy.

But things change around the age of three. Becky's world of understanding grows rapidly. She reaches a milestone in her cognitive development. She has a new awareness and growing understanding of life outside of herself. Until a child satisfactorily reaches this stage, parents can only manage outward behavior. You might be managing behavior with moral implications in mind, thus sowing good seeds of right behavior, but your efforts of helping the child internalize moral precepts will not take place until the conscience awakens and joins itself to moral understanding.

When this milestone is crossed, parents embark on a new pathway of training that continues for the next twelve to fifteen years. You begin transitioning from controlling outward behavior only to proactively shaping inner attitudes and heart responses. You are now actively shaping the conscience that will rule your child the rest of his life.

Here's the transition—the following springtime, Becky and Mom are strolling through the park and come upon the same border of tulips. Attracted by the colors, Becky moves closer to touch one and then contemplates picking one. Now she hears her guardian's voice (conscience) say, "No, Becky. We do not pick flowers in the public garden," followed by this moral explanation: "Becky, those flowers are here for everyone to enjoy and to be shared by all. If each person picked a flower, there would be none for others to enjoy."

Please note this transition carefully. Mom's guiding restraint came first to two-year-old Becky: "No, Becky, do not pick flowers . . ." (control of outward behavior), then followed by the moral reason,

"Flowers are here to be shared by everyone" (introduction of an otherness ethic). The knowledge of why flowers should not be picked from public gardens serves to guide three-year-old Becky's future responses. Thus, the transition from external to internal authority takes place. Please note—this is a process that takes place over time as more deposits are made into Becky's moral account.

Similar scenarios will be repeated a number of different times and ways throughout Becky's early years. Becky is now learning many moral truths and otherness virtues. The emphasis is not only on what Becky shouldn't do, but also on what she should do. Like a single bank account, all deposits end up in one place. That place is called the conscience.

How Does the Human Conscience Work?

The human conscience actually functions at two levels of existence— a *lower* and *higher* conscience. The lower conscience contains an innate *sense* of right and wrong, which all humanity shares. The higher conscience is subject to training and receives the specific *standards* of right and wrong formed by beliefs and values.

While this chapter deals specifically with the higher conscience, there is a fascinating account about the lower conscience contained in the early writings of the Hebrew Bible. In the fourth chapter of the first book, God pronounced a curse on Cain for the murder of his brother Abel. He was to become a vagrant and a wanderer of the earth. Cain responded, "Whoever finds me will kill me."[3] Here we see the lower conscience operating. How did Cain know others would

---

[3]See Genesis 4:14, *The New Geneva Study Bible* (Nashville: Thomas Nelson), 1982.

require his life as a result of killing his brother? No law at that time had been established. Even God acknowledges the probability of that action by marking him as "one not to be touched."[4] Cain was operating off his innate sense of right and wrong. Here is a story over five thousand years old reflecting an anthropological description of mankind then and now.

Much more central to parenting a preschooler is the function of the higher conscience (also referred to as the heart of a child, heart of man, the moral conscience, and the trainable conscience). Aristotle acknowledged and pointed out the trainable side of the human conscience. It is here that the knowledge and standards of right and wrong are written on the heart. It is the place where values, virtues, prohibitions, and moral initiatives are located. In the illustration above, Becky's Mom made a deposit in Becky's conscience by giving her the moral reason for not picking flowers in public places. The specific elements of right and wrong were deposited into Becky's higher conscience, connecting with a group of otherness virtues.

All parents have a social obligation to train their children in community values. With their moral pen they write a prescription of right and wrong, what to do and what not to do, and all the moral reasons why or why not. Since parents offer instruction both by precept and example, attention must be paid not only to *what* moral truth is imparted to a child, but *how* it is imparted. This point will be demonstrated later in a very tangible way and is more fully developed in the following book in this series, *On Becoming Childwise*.

The rest of this chapter is devoted to explaining how the conscience actually functions. What are the parts? How do they work

---

[4]See Genesis 4:15, *The New Geneva Study Bible* (Nashville: Thomas Nelson), 1982.

together? What role do parents play in shaping the conscience? Our discussion centers on four activities:

- Establishing the Moral Warehouse
- The Activities of the Conscience
- The Moral Search Mechanism
- Signs of a Healthy and Unhealthy Conscience

Establishing the Moral Warehouse

The ability to receive and store moral principles speaks to the capacity of the conscience. Every person of normal birth possesses this capacity. It is the place were parents make deposits of moral knowledge. You are constantly teaching your child in many different ways, in a number of differing contexts throughout the day. You instruct your child to share, be kind, tell the truth, be patient, ask nicely, be polite, show respect, act courteously, and say please and thank you. This is a process that takes place day in and day out, week by week, and year by year. Believe it or not, those moral impressions are going somewhere. They are stored in the child's moral warehouse—the conscience.

We have all seen them—those large metal warehouses. Imagine one standing in a field. You step through the roll-up door onto a glistening smooth floor. Aisles of metal shelving are neatly arranged for easy access. You can see that some shelves are filled with various virtues while others are spilling over with admirable character qualities. You recognize each of these items because you the parent dutifully and purposely placed them there. On one shelf rests your teaching about kindness. On another, the various forms of honesty, and down the aisle there is a group of virtues that demonstrate respect: for elders, parents, teachers, and authority. Not far from there are the virtues of sharing, kind speech, and self-control. Each is marked with a dangling red identification tag making these virtues easy to find and retrieve. This is a picture of your child's moral warehouse—his conscience. Some shelves are still bare, waiting for future instruction in virtues, others shelves are filled to capacity..

In child training, the management rights to that warehouse belong to parents. You are the managers of your child's conscience. You have the marking pen. You write the values on their hearts. Some parents do this with fervency and intent while others take a nonchalant approach. Fervency is highly preferred. As the shelves begin to fill, the four activities of the conscience can start their work.

The Four Activities of the Conscience

Remember Becky from our previous story? Now eight years old, she hopped from bed early—eager to finish her painting-by-numbers started the night before. It only came to a halt because Mom insisted that it was time for Becky to go to bed. Mom also instructed Becky to complete her morning routine before she reopened her paints. But Mom is still sleeping and ... Becky's rational thoughts faded to silence as another voice, that "special something" voice began to speak. Guidelines for morning activities were clearly established in Becky's home. Knowing her bed must be made, hair brushed, and other responsibilities performed before she was free, Becky swiftly worked through these tasks in hopes of getting to her project before breakfast. This eight-year-old's conscience monitored her activity and redirected her energy to accomplish what was required. The process began years ago, when she was a preschooler taking a walk in a garden of tulips.

The conscience has the ability to assess behavior in any moment and render judicial opinions, either by accusing or defending one's actions. Accusing speaks to the negative side of the conscience, while defending speaks to the positive side. When we say our conscience accuses us, we are referring to its ability to make a judgment on a potential moral violation based on what is in the warehouse. The conscience (that inward voice) warns man when he is about to do wrong. If he does not heed that warning, his conscience will accuse him. This is done through the mechanism of guilt.

Guilt, shame, and empathy are moral emotions common to the human experience. Any attempt to get rid of guilt is an attempt to get rid of the conscience. Guilt is not a condition of the healthy or the sick, but of right versus wrong. When we cross the boundary of our own conscience, guilt is activated. We did something we knew we shouldn't have. Guilt is there to remind us to take care of our misdeeds. If a person never experiences guilt, either his conscience has been hardened, or he has an empty warehouse desperately in need of filling.

The good news is found in the positive function of the human conscience. The conscience will also prompt us to do right and confirms us when we do. For example, you see a crumpled piece of paper lying in the hallway. You sense a prompting from within—"Pick up the paper even though you didn't drop it." You do and suddenly that feeling of "rightness" comes over you. That sense, that you complied with the integrity of your heart, is your conscience saying, "You did the right thing."

So the conscience will prompt us to do right and then confirms us when we do. It also warns us of potential wrong and then accuses us if we cross the line. For example, a gum wrapper casually slips from your hand. Even as your feet move forward, a thousand impulses begin to prompt you to stop. "Guilty! Guilty!" Your conscience screams, until you glance around to see if anyone else can hear it. The next question is—How is this possible? Why is *my* conscience bothered by *my* behavior? Here is how it works.

The Moral Search Mechanism

The four activities of the conscience—prompting, confirming, warning, and accusing, operate in harmony with the values stored in the warehouse. The conscience also has the ability to monitor the moral horizon and alert one to potential ethical situations possibly in need of a response. Once alerted to a need, the prompting or warning mechanism moves us to action.

Every day we participate in numerous potential ethical situations. Whether you're shopping, sitting in class, doing laundry, driving home, watching television, sitting in the grandstands of your child's soccer match, or chewing gum—you are constantly confronted with ethical circumstances challenging the values in your warehouse. The moral search mechanism, like a continuous scanning radar beam, looks over the horizon, taking in data, evaluating it for moral liability, and then responds by going to the moral warehouse in search of a value or virtue to act on.

The search mechanism, like a busy, bright red R2D2 robot begins moving up and down the aisles, searching each shelf. It is looking to see if there is a corresponding value in need of satisfying. If it finds many or just one, it pulls it off the shelf and immediately returns to posted sentries on guard, warning and prompting. The robot than takes the value and waves it in front of the sentries, demanding, "You need to do something about this!" Of course, if nothing is found on the warehouse shelves, the search ends and nothing happens.

At a private memorial service, an elderly pastor stepped into the room, joining the men and women already gathered in the prayer chamber. All the seats were taken, and one could not help but notice that this senior saint needed a place to rest. In the back of the room, at least one young man's search mechanism, found in his conscience, was on the move. The situation for him presented a moral dilemma— elderly pastor; chair needed. This information was sent through the warehouse carried by the search engine robot. Scanning the aisle look-ing for related values, the robot pinpointed two red tagged virtues needing consideration. One was labeled "Respect and honor age." The second file carried the heading "Preferring others over oneself."

Lifting these values off the shelf, the robot, lights flashing, rushes back to the conscience waving the files, announcing, "These values need attention!" The *prompting* mechanism says, "Honor this man by offering your seat." The *warning* mechanism replies, "You are dishon-oring age by ignoring this man's need for a seat." Both mechanisms call for a moral solution. In response, the younger man rises, greets the elderly pastor, and offers his seat. The gentleman accepts. This action satisfied the moral standard written on the young man's heart, prompting the right response. That is how it works.

You have a search mechanism operating in your warehouse. You know the sensation of the prompting to do what is right, and you are familiar with the sensation of warning when you are about to do something you know is wrong. Both sets of feelings operate in con-junction with your moral warehouse and the values and virtues placed there. But what happens when a person grows up without sufficient moral guidance?

Let me add a little twist to the true-life experience illustrated above. What if, as a child, that young man's parents never emphasized the value of respecting age or preferring others? Would respect for age be naturally present? We're afraid not. The search mechanism begins its scan of the aisle. Not finding a corresponding value tagged "Respect Age," it returns empty-handed. There is no prompting or warning because nothing is found.

What does that mean for parents today? If there is no principle to stir the child's heart, the child stays morally immature, either becoming the victim or the bully because of his lack of social discernment. There is truth to the old proverb that says, "For as a man thinks in his heart, so is he."[5] Our life is the product of what is in our hearts. And what is in the heart of a child is the product of parents putting their moral convictions into their child's moral warehouse.

The only difference between you and your child's conscience is the amount and complexity of the resident life values. Children start with a simple sense of right and wrong that grows into a complex moral scheme reflective of the home and society at large.

Signs of a Healthy and Unhealthy Conscience

Positive and *prohibitive* are terms describing conditions of the heart as a result of right or wrong training. The healthy, *positive* conscience says, "I ought to do this because it is right," or, "I ought not do this because it is wrong." The *prohibitive* conscience says, "I must or else

---

[5] See Proverbs 23:7, *The New Geneva Study Bible* (Nashville: Thomas Nelson), 1982.

I'll be punished." With the latter, the motivation to do right is not because of the love of virtue but rather because the individual fears reproof or punishment.

Positive development takes place when parents build into their child's conscience the reason *why* "right is right" and "wrong is wrong." A child will develop a healthy conscience when his parents are good models of the qualities they desire to see in their child and when they encourage the child to do right as opposed to only discouraging him from doing wrong. Such a child sees obedience as attractive, not as a distasteful action done merely to avoid punitive retaliation for failure to comply.

The prohibitive conscience is not a guilty conscience, but an ongoing state of potential guilt. The person who lives this way has not necessarily done anything wrong, but lives his life as if he were always on the verge of doing wrong or constantly worries that others will think he is doing something wrong. In this case, doing wrong is the overly sensitive fear of disappointing someone, being misunderstood, or being rejected if he or she does not conform. Practically, this results in the coward that dies a thousand deaths. He may do many virtuous acts, but not out of love of what is right, rather out of fear of rejection. Here are some of the ways parents instill a prohibitive conscience in their children.

- Parents manipulate their child by creating the fear of losing Mom or Dad's love. Conditional love then becomes the motivator for right behavior.
- Parents manipulate the conscience by making their child feel guilty. For the child, avoiding guilt becomes the motivator for right behavior.

- Parents fail to provide the moral reasons for behavior. As a result, the constant fear of punishment, reproof, and rejection—not the love of virtue—becomes the motivation for right behavior.

The one who lives with the fear of potential guilt (i.e., potential rejection for wrong decisions) does not work from a pure heart. Virtues become burdensome, and a life of moral freedom is nonexistent. The effects of a prohibitive conscience can be lifelong. Do you have a conscience like that? Take this subjective test, and then score yourself. Many parents find this self-evaluation helpful in understanding what makes them tick from a moral standpoint. This test serves only as a guide to gain understanding of your own heart with the hope that you will better appreciate what must be put into your child's heart.

Prohibitive Conscience Test

Scale: 1 = Never true of me
        3 = Sometimes true of me
        5 = True 50 percent of the time/Not true 50 percent of the time
        7 = Usually true of me
       10 = Always true of me

(If a question does not apply, think of how you might respond.)

1.___ When someone says, "I need to talk to you right away," I get nervous and begin to wonder what I did wrong.

2.____ Even as an adult, somehow I am made to feel guilty by my mother or father if I do not do what she or he asks or demands.

3.____ Somehow my mother-in-law/father-in-law make(s) me feel guilty if I do not do what she or he asks or demands.

4.____ If fifty people told me I did a good job but one person did not like what I did and was critical of me, the discouragement from the one person would be greater than the encouragement of the fifty.

5.____ Sometimes I participate in activities or attend functions even when I do not want to, just out of the fear that someone might say something about me if I were not there.

6.____ When I am in a disagreement with another person, I tend to give in and say to myself, "It really doesn't matter anyway."

7.____ I tend to worry about saying something that might be misunderstood or misconstrued.

8.____ When I'm asked to help a friend or relative and I need to say no for legitimate reasons, I still feel guilty.

9.____ I am the one who usually says, "I'm sorry."

10.____ I fear losing my child's love when I discipline him or her.

Scoring the prohibitive conscience test (if all ten questions were answered) is based on average responses:

76 –100 Excessively high prohibitive conscience

61 – 75 Seriously high prohibitive conscience

46 – 60 High prohibitive conscience

35 – 45 Low prohibitive conscience

25 – 34 Healthy conscience

10 – 24 Moving toward a hardened conscience

What Can I Do about My Prohibitive Conscience?

If you have trouble with a prohibitive and fearful conscience, the first step of correction is acknowledging that you do have a problem. To use a computer analogy—you have corrupt data in need of fixing. Here is a simple three-step process to get you started:

- Please see comments in Appendix B. Take special note of the section dealing with "Beliefs and Goals." Establish in writing what you believe to be the driving truths in your life.
- Moral sensibility is an antidote to a prohibitive conscience. The deeper your understanding of *why* "right is right" and "wrong is wrong," the calmer the troubled waters of moral experience will become. Some of the most fearful people in the world are those who do all the right things but do not know *why* they are the right things to do. As a result, they tend to second-guess every decision they make.

• Next, if a prohibitive conscience controls your behavior, then you need to start taking control now. Resolve not to automatically respond to the situations you face day by day. Instead, think about what moral principles should govern your response. Train yourself to be driven by virtue and moral reason, not fear. Whatever the reason for this behavior, the cycle can and must stop with you.

As we stated above, the person who lives with a prohibitive conscience has not necessarily done anything wrong but lives his life as if he were always on the verge of doing wrong or constantly worried that others will think he has done something wrong. That is a terrible weight to carry in life and a burden that you do not want to pass on to your children. Because children learn by imitation and absorb subtle attitudes as quickly as a dry sponge does water, getting your own heart right is a prerequisite to helping your child get his heart right. You can do it, and for the sake of your children, you must do it!

Chapter Four

The Choice Addiction

*D*oes this happen in your home? It is breakfast time, and four-year-old Jackson enters the kitchen. You have just poured orange juice in the red cup. When Jackson notices, he politely reminds you that his cup is the blue one with the starship. You smile and make the switch. He also informs you of his desire to have grape juice this morning instead of orange juice. "No problem," you think. "Both are healthy." You pour the orange juice in your glass and the grape juice in his. As you begin to butter Jackson's toast, he decides that today he would like jam instead of butter. Well, the buttered toast can be for Mom. You put another slice of bread into the toaster for Jackson. Putting jam on it is no big deal.

After breakfast, it is reading time. You say to Jackson, "Sit here near the light, and Mom wants to read you a story." But Jackson decides to sit near the big pillow. The big pillows are fun, so mom joins Jackson. Next, you pick up a book and open it on your lap. Jackson, however, picks another story, his favorite, and then the two of you enjoy a fifteen-minute adventure. After reading time, your son informs you, "Mom, I'm going to play on my swing set," and off he goes. "Okay," you say as he disappears out the door. "Thanks for letting me know."

So far the morning has been rather easy—no conflicts or trials. Who said parenting was hard? At noon you instruct Jackson to put away his toys and get ready for lunch. "Mommy," Jackson says, "I decided to have lunch later. I'm playing with my trucks now." You repeat your instructions with a little more authority. Jackson is equally firm. Things begin to escalate. Soon your little tempest becomes a raging storm; a small skirmish becomes a full-blown battle of the wills. Frustrated and discouraged, you ask yourself, "Why am I experiencing such behavior from my son? After all, have I not been fair with him all morning, meeting his needs and desires? Why am I getting such defiance and resistance to my instructions? This choice thing is not working like the experts said it would."

Let's look back over the morning from another perspective. Who decided that it would be the blue cup and not the red cup? The child did. Who decided it would be grape juice and not orange juice? The child did. Who decided that it would be jam instead of butter? Again, the child made this decision. Who decided where he would sit and what he would read? The child. Who decided what happened after reading time? The child also made this decision.

Jackson has been making every decision for himself. He has gotten his way all day long. He is lord of all he surveys and master of his own destiny. Every time Mom wants X, Jackson chooses Y, and so Mom changes to Y. Jackson may even change to Z. So why on earth should he think Mom had any voice in the matter whatsoever? Mom's desires for him are merely suggestions or points of departure. What's up with this?

For Jackson, and children like him, having the final word is a way of life. Mom's instructions are an intrusion. At the ripe old age of four years, Jackson has become *wise in his own eyes*. He is so used to making all of the decisions in his life that any change on Mom's part is worthy of resistance. This false sense of empowerment and the accompanying feeling of self-reliance gets children into trouble. Children who are *wise in their own eyes* will tend to go places they should not go and say things they should not say.

At this age, Jackson is not able to discriminate between *nonmoral* choices (the red cup versus the blue cup) and *moral* choices that require obedience. From his perspective, saying no to Mom's instructions is no different than saying no to her selection of juice. The privilege of refusing the orange juice is transferred to the right to refuse any of Mom's instructions. Consequently, Mom has a problem. The observation that "Absolute power corrupts absolutely" is true even in children.

Getting to the Root of the Problem

All too often, parents rush the process of growing up. Too soon, Dad and Grandpa are signing R. J. up for junior hockey, simply because he was mesmerized by the latest ESPN commercial. He slides on the polished floor with a plastic sword as a makeshift hockey stick, and Dad has him at the ice rink three mornings a week. Never mind the fact that R. J. is only four years old and hates the cold. Dad is left coercing, correcting, pleading, and dealing with tears, while R. J. is clearly out of his league. R. J. simply doesn't care about a future contract in the NHL. Poor R. J.—none of this frustration needed to be in his life.

To summarize, R. J.'s dad placed him in a situation bigger than his four-year-old mental or physical capacities can manage. Dad wants him to be like the big kids on the ice and finds himself trying to correct a problem that should never have existed in the first place. R. J. is not interested in competitive hockey.

Maybe you have not rushed your child to the hockey rink lately, but have you rushed him in other behavioral activities that are way beyond his intellectual and social readiness or interest? Your eighteen-month-old points to a baboon on the T.V. screen and you're thinking how to best prepare him for zoological studies at Harvard. Before you rush to the primate section of the local library or rush your preschooler off to a week of math camp for the intellectually gifted, think about his readiness to learn. While it is true that the brain grows best when challenged, it is also true that such challenges must be developmentally and age appropriate. Too often parents push their children into higher learning activities only to discover that their children's abilities are impaired because they were rushed.

In our sophisticated society, we tend to rush our children (or more accurately in some cases, bulldoze them) beyond their developmental schedules. Children in our society are rushed morally, behaviorally, sexually, intellectually, and physically. We either give them too much information or too many freedoms of self-governance, far beyond their intellectual, moral, and behavioral readiness. Like R. J.'s Dad, many parents push their children into activities that are more often a parental fantasy than the child's dream. Three-year-old children playing organized soccer, complete with shin guards and body armor, is a bit much. In these cases, the driving force behind the competition comes almost entirely from the parents.

A second and more subtle way to push our children too quickly in development is to flood them with far too many choices and to give them too much freedom to make decisions. Jackson is a product of this type of parenting. He gets to choose when to snack, when to nap, when to play, what to watch, what to wear, when to come, and when to go. Such freedoms in self-governance are as dangerous as rushing children into sports or academic activities before their little brains and bodies are sufficiently organized to master the tasks.

Giving too many choices too early pushes children way outside the funnel in the diagram introduced in *On Becoming Toddlerwise*. This is evident in Jackson's life. Conflict results because the child cannot handle the power associated with decision-making freedoms prior to the establishment of a self-regulating, moral conscience.

Why do some parents face greater behavioral deficits in their children than other parents do? Why do some children tend to bounce from one activity to another, never fulfilled with any? Why do some children challenge their parents on everything—morning, noon, and night? Before we blame ADD, ADHD, ODD, junk food, or bad genes, we might first consider if this child is being parented "outside the funnel." If this is the case, the good news is that there is a nonmedical cure. Such behavioral problems can be fixed.

Parenting outside the Funnel

Childhood experts agree that when a child is at peace with his environment, his learning potential increases, learning disorders abate, and dysfunctional behaviors diminish. So what happens when a child is consistently placed in an environment that is not age appropriate? What does it do to a child if she is always smaller than the chairs, the toilets, and the other kids? What does it do if she's always larger? What happens to a child who is given too many freedoms, too early? What about a child who is free to direct his own life without parental accountability?

Once again, we find it helpful to return to the funnel diagram introduced in *On Becoming Toddlerwise*. In this diagram the narrow stem represents the early stages of parenting, when the child is very young. The wider part represents the expanding growth, maturity, and gradual freedoms a child is able to handle.

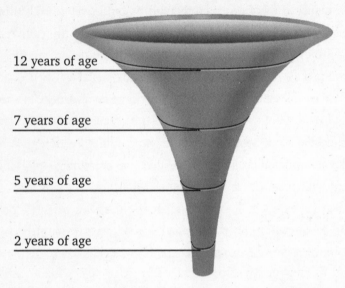

12 years of age

7 years of age

5 years of age

2 years of age

In their all-too-complex worlds, parents tend to rush their children through childhood. They do this when they parent outside the funnel. In an effort to give the child confidence, parents sometimes allow their child behaviors or freedoms that are neither age appropriate nor in harmony with the child's moral and intellectual capabilities.

To allow a three-year-old child the freedoms appropriate to a six-year-old child, for example, is to parent outside the funnel. It forces a child to carry an oversized burden he is not prepared to carry. Contrary to child-centered thinking, such freedoms do not facilitate healthy learning patterns. Instead, they create oversized problems for an undersized child. Please note that the problem does not start with the child. It begins with the parents, who have thrust their child into a situation bigger than he can handle at his age. Often, parents do not realize they are allowing this to happen. Let's say that six-year-old Kyle wants to watch a cartoon on television that features high-kicking action super-heros. At six years of age, Kyle can handle the stimulation that comes from watching this type of show (for one half hour). Kyle's three-year-old brother, Tyler, wanders into the room and settles down to watch the same program. Soon, Mom is having to intervene as Tyler is now karate-kicking his brother in the face. Unless an older sibling is willing to watch a program geared towards a younger child, it is rare that it is appropriate for children in different phases of maturity to view television together. It is common for parents to miss this.

Big Britches and Wise Eyes

No concerned parent would give a three-year-old child a sharp knife and let him peel his own apple. But most parents would consider granting that freedom to their twelve-year-old. The difference, obviously, is in regard to the age and sense of responsibility in the children.

As parents, we are very protective of our children when it comes to health and safety issues. We would never let our four-year-old child climb a ladder leaning against the second-story window. Nor would we intentionally put our children in dangerous environments. We would not let our five-year-old child spray weed poison around the house just because it looks like fun. If we granted such freedoms on a regular basis, our children would probably assume a false sense of confidence in their own abilities and judgments. It is that unjustified confidence that can lead to reckless behavior and tragedy.

When was the last time you heard these clichés: "That kid is too big for his britches," or, "That child is a smarty-pants, and it is going to get her in trouble one of these days"? Beneath these less-than-complimentary statements is a legitimate concern that warns against creating the false impression in the mind of a child that she is able to do anything, say anything, and go anywhere without parental guidance or approval. Simply put, this is a child who has been granted too many freedoms of self-governance too early.

It is our firm conviction, based on our observations, that more conflicts arise out of this *wise in your own eyes* attitude than any other single factor in parenting. A child who acts *wise in his own eyes* is a child living above his age appropriate level of freedom. He is living and playing outside the funnel, wrongly assuming rights of self-rule and direction.

How does it happen? What are some of the ways children become *wise in their own eyes* and thus acquire a false sense of security? Here are the three most common ways during the preschool years:

- Parents grant too many decision-making freedoms.
- Parents grant too many physical freedoms.
- Parents grant too many verbal freedoms.

Decision-Making Freedoms—Too Many Choices, Too Early

The cry of our day revolves around choices. "Give children plenty of choices in the early years," says the theorist. "Let the child decide, and he will learn to make wise decisions when he grows up." However, that outcome may not be sustained by evidence. Our prisons are full of people who made choices all their lives. Contrary to the theorist's opinion, having choices and the freedom to be self-determining does not mean people will make the right choices.

There is no question that children can be guided into good patterns of decision-making by learning how to make wise choices as children. Allowing a child to make his own decisions is both educational and rewarding. However, good decision-making skills do not rely on the natural inclination of the child, but instead upon careful parental guidance. It is crucial for parents to take leadership in this matter. Without guidance, the child will grow up making decisions based only on his natural inclinations: pursuing pleasure and avoiding pain.

Here, too, parenting philosophies help or hinder the development of wise decision making. Neither overcontrolling nor undercontrolling methods are helpful approaches for teaching choices. The first tends to deny the child sufficient opportunities to make choices. This suppresses the child's age-appropriate sense of control and the educational opportunities to learn through wise and unwise decisions. The second philosophy overindulges the child with too many choices, too early.

As it relates to decision-making freedoms, the majority of parents today are not guilty of overly suppressing a child's choices. On the contrary, most homes tend to go in the opposite direction. At a typical three-year-old child's birthday party, guests are offered multiple beverage selections before they even sit down. And then they have to choose between napkin colors, fork colors, plate styles, the size of their piece of cake, and whether they want a corner or middle piece.

Please keep this in perspective. We are not saying you should hold back all choices from your children. We are suggesting that you guard against prematurely granting freedoms to decide on issues that your child is not developmentally, intellectually, or emotionally able to handle. Let's face it, making decisions all day can be overwhelming to adults. Think how this affects very young children. They might be willing to go along with this freedom you have given them, but the stress it causes them will show up in a child's attitude. And think about this—if a child is ready to make choices about major life issues, why does he need Mom and Dad around?

Freedoms from a Child's Perspective

Remember, the real problem is not in giving children choices, but doing so prematurely and to the point of overindulgence. Is this true in your family? This can be easily measured with a simple question or two. Can your child handle not being given a choice of what to eat at breakfast? Will she go ballistic if she cannot pick out her own play clothes for the day?

Parents can know if their child is addicted to choice by simply observing what happens when all choices are taken away. For example, if at breakfast Mom offers milk in a clear glass, cereal in a plain bowl, and a piece of buttered toast on a plate, would your child accept this without complaint?

Try it tomorrow morning. If he comes to the table and accepts your meal decision without complaining or protesting, then your child is probably able to handle a degree of freedom in decision making in this area. If, on the other hand, your child protests your breakfast selection, grumbles, complains, cries, or refuses to eat, you may have a problem. There is a strong possibility that you have a child who is addicted to choice.

A child who is addicted to choice cannot emotionally cope in life when no choice is available to him. That is what happened to Jackson. He recoiled when confronted with required behavior because he was addicted to self-determination. Therein lies the sad legacy of poorly thought-out parenting philosophies. Jackson's parents set him up for frustration and emotional danger while thinking they were helping him to succeed.

Does your preschooler fall apart when you deny him an impulsive desire? Does he debate you all the time; must he have the last word? Does he always have a better idea? When you give specific instructions, does your child struggle to submit, or give you less than you asked? Consider the possibility that he is addicted to deciding for himself—he is addicted to choice. You may have given him too many freedoms, too early.

This is no way to prepare him for life. The real world will not bow to his every whim, nor will it always give choices. You are not doing anyone—yourself, the child, or society—any favors by allowing him to be addicted to choice.

More Signs of Trouble—Verbal and Physical Freedoms

Do you let your three-year-old child go into the backyard to play without asking permission? Do you let your five-year-old daughter decide for herself when she can go next door to play with her friend? Think through your day. How many times do you hear your child say, "Mom, I'm going to…" rather than, "Mom, *may* I…?" Is your child asking your permission to do things, or just telling you what he is going to do?

How we speak to our children and how we allow them to speak

to us greatly affect patterns of behavior. Again, remember that this chapter is devoted to prevention. We want to prevent poor behavior by what we do and say. What we say and what we allow our child to say to us represents verbal definitions of the boundaries of the child's perception of self, including self-reliance and self-governance.

The child who customarily tells you what she is going to do is assuming a level of decision-making freedom that she may or may not have. And if this continues, it is because her parents have allowed her to take this ground and hold it. Parents must evaluate whether the freedom to decide the matter in question is age appropriate.

If your five-year-old girl believes she has the freedom to come and go at will, then what will stop her from wandering off when you are together at the playground, at the mall, or at the beach? It is not just the wandering off that is our concern, but the child's confirmed sense of independence from parental guidance at such a tender age. This is another type of freedom that can push the child outside the funnel.

There is nothing wrong with a child wanting to go next door to play. Nor is there anything inherently wrong with a parent choosing to grant such a desire. The problem concerns whether it is the child or the parent who is ultimately making the decisions.

There is a simple technique you can use to keep this problem at bay. Have your child ask permission rather than informing you of his decision. Have your child say, "Mom, may I go…?" rather than, "Mom, I'm going…" Young children need more from their parents than simply guidance. They also need the security that parental leadership brings into their world. Seeking permission helps a child realize his dependence on your leadership. It also helps prevent a child from becoming wise in his own eyes.

One warning: this technique will only work if you actually fulfill your parental role. If your child asks permission to go next door, and you say no, you may witness a case of spontaneous combustion right there in your living room. If your child throws a tantrum (or threatens to in front of guests) and you give in, you have not made an adjustment at all. The child is still telling you what he is going to do. You have only changed the vocabulary.

If a child never has to ask for permission, he will rightly assume that it means he has the freedom to do whatever he wants, whenever he wants to, regardless of ownership or ability. How many of these children we see in society today! Shopping malls, amusement parks, and airports are full of them. A child who never has to ask permission functions without restraint. And that is something you would never want to wish on any child, least of all yours.

Verbal freedoms are more than just a child claiming his right to come and go at will. It is also a problem of tone. Listen to the way your child talks to you and to others. Is he characterized by being bossy? How does his tone sound? Is he rude to his siblings? Does he always need to have the last word? Is his speech demanding? "Mommy, now! I want it right now!" Does he routinely tell you no, leaving you to wonder who's really in charge? These are all classic signs of a child with too many verbal freedoms.

If your child lives under the impression that he is a verbal peer with you, your instructions and desire for compliance move from a "need-to-do" list to a "wish list." Mom and Dad, let us remind you that *you* are the parents. Control the tone that flows from your precious child's little lips.

Fixing this problem requires pulling in the verbal boundaries. (Don't worry. You will not be stifling your child's freedom of expression, just modifying the character behind it.) Here again is that workable, but simple solution: Insist that the child respond "Yes, Mommy," or "Yes, Daddy."

If you are in the retraining process, and you know that your child is going to verbally battle your every request, then establish in your instructions the parameters of his response. "Timmy, Mommy wants you to pick up your toys now. And Timmy, Mommy wants to hear a 'Yes, Mommy.'"

"But, but, but—"

"No, Timmy. 'Yes, Mommy' is the only response you are allowed to give me right now."

"Yes, Mommy."

Other mothers have approached this challenge in the following way. If Timmy answers with, "But, but, but," Mom can say, "Timmy, you do not have the freedom to talk back to your mother."

Add some resolve to your request, and the problem is usually fixed fairly quickly. The new habit of speech begins to override the old.

That's Me! What Can I Do?

If you find yourself somewhere in this chapter, don't despair! Choice addictions are treatable. First, evaluate just how bad the addiction is. From mealtime to reading time to bedtime, are you continually offering choices? Is it a way of life for you and your child? Is the choice problem multiplied by too many verbal and physical freedoms on the part of your child?

Second, get the whole family to work together on limiting any of the three problems mentioned above. You must narrow the boundaries. One way to do this is to take back ownership of those freedoms you have given out prematurely. Instead of letting your four-year-old son decide what he will have for breakfast, you decide. Instead of giving him the freedom to decide when to come and go, you start directing him. Our next chapter is a great place to start. Start adding some structure to your child's day. If your child is four or five years old, consider sitting him down and explaining what you are up to. "Jackson, Mom has been letting you make all your decisions. From now on, Mom will start helping you make them. Some days, I will ask you what you want for breakfast. Other days, Mommy will pick for you. The same goes for what you are going to wear, what you are going to watch, and how you are going to play."

The breakfast conversation might sound something like this:

"Jackson, today you are having cereal for breakfast."

"But Mom, I want pancakes!"

"No. Breakfast today is Mom's decision. Jackson, I would like to hear a 'Yes, Mommy' from you."

"Yes, Mommy."

There will be days when the child can choose, especially as he demonstrates contentment with you being in charge. But right now you must take back ownership of this vitally important lost ground. You can give him back the freedom to choose after he has learned to accept your choices without insurrection—or even grumbling or whining. Most days, you or your spouse will decide what is for dinner, what is to be worn, when there will be organized playtime, and when it is time to come inside. You want your children to find wisdom in your leadership and to avoid becoming wise in their own eyes.

But what happens when your child throws a fit because he did not get his sugar-laden Choco-Bombs? How do you handle correction in that moment when you are just starting to reclaim this territory? The answer is—do nothing, nothing at all. Consider this moment a chance to take inventory of just how deeply seated the addiction is. Your natural temptation will be to try to fix the problem right in that moment. But if you do, expect that both you and your child will have a miserable day. You must do more than fix the moment. You must change the child's perspective (and maybe your own) on your right to rule and guide his young life.

Starting Over

When should you attempt to make some changes? First, finish reading this book. Then go back all the way to the beginning of this series in Chapter One, *A Baby Needs a Family*, of *On Becoming Babywise*. Do you remember couch-time? Get with your spouse on the couch every day for fifteen minutes together. Begin creating a new impression for your child of what Mom and Dad are about. "Hey, they aren't just my overindulgent caregivers; they are a team committed to loving each other and me—not just me, me, me."

A review of Chapter Six, *Conflict, Training, and Instruction*, in *On Becoming Toddlerwise* will also help. See how you are doing with your verbal instructions and your child's response. Start working on the "Yes, Mom" and "Yes, Dad" response. Do not underestimate the power of this response in retraining your child's heart. It actually creates a willingness in your child to follow your lead.

Of course, be consistent. Reclaiming leadership in your home— breaking the addiction to choosing—can take anywhere from three days to three weeks or more. Changing ingrained patterns of behavior takes time. But children are resilient. In their hearts, they want to be led.

Once Upon a Time in Real Life

The letter below summarizes just how fast a turnaround you might experience:

Mr. Ezzo,

I wanted to tell you how the "addicted to choice" material has impacted our three-year-old daughter. This information came to us at a most opportune time. Our daughter was beginning to have uncharacteristic temper tantrums. She had two fits in which she was throwing things, hitting, kicking, screaming. Way out of character for our little girl.

When I found your material on choices, I started paying attention at home. I noticed that both my wife and I offered her choices on almost everything. My wife would regularly fix our daughter special meals if she thought she wouldn't like what we were having. Our little girl got to choose what she was going to wear, what she was going to play, etc.

I told my wife about your choice addiction idea, and she wanted to try your advice. When she told me about the second tantrum, I decided it was time for a change. We explained to our daughter what we were going to do and then radically restricted her choices.

Something amazing has happened: Our daughter is much happier. She's sleeping better, eating better, and behaving better. It's almost as if she is glad to have the limits. I expected her behavior to improve and the tantrums to stop, but I didn't expect her to enjoy the restrictions. She even reminds us if we give her a choice she feels she shouldn't have!

Summary

Prevention is the best form of correction. You should continually evaluate what you allow your child to do and whether those freedoms are appropriate considering his age, understanding, and abilities. Are you giving him inappropriate freedoms? Let freedoms be handed out carefully as the child demonstrates contentment with your authority and shows responsibility in previously given freedoms. Granting freedoms consistent with a child's level of self-control equals developmental harmony.

Chapter Five

Structuring Your Preschooler's Day

Carla Link, Contributor

H ere we go again! Two-year-old Kaitlin finally settles down for her nap just when it's time to pick up four-year-old Michael from preschool. Once that child hits the deck, all hope is gone for the day. Between constant demands for Mom to play, endless snacks, and trails of toys scattered around the house, Denise is looking to the sky for the elite rescue force she once saw in a Star Wars movie. Meanwhile, the dog paid a visit to the neighbor's trash can, which now lays on its side spewing tissues and shoe boxes all over the street. In the back of her mind, Denise ponders the deeper issues: Is there really a rule about having dinner *every* night? If so, do cheesecake and toast qualify? Most importantly, with the house a mess, bills to pay, and mountains of laundry piling up— will my head ever hit the soft, downy comfort of my beckoning bed? This woman is in despair. Nothing in itself is a huge hurdle—it's the zillion little obstacles she faces every day that make her feel more like a prisoner of random chaos than like a mother on a beautiful mission of raising children.

Parenting resources? Oh, Denise has plenty of those. Books, magazines, and Internet articles decorate the library, kitchen counter, and bedroom nightstand. Like many of her peers, Denise believes that the more information she has about children, their natures, phases of growth, and skill levels, the better equipped she will be for the task of mothering. Alas, if only she had energy enough to read any of them, she might figure out this kid thing once and for all. Each night, she resolves that tomorrow will be a good day to delve into the world of childhood experts.

In part, her procrastination is rooted in the fear of confusion. Won't all these self-proclaimed experts contradict each other with their diverse views marketed to young parents? She's been that route already, trying one thing, like child massage to calm Kaitlin for a nap or the old standby "count down" to get Michael's attention. A few days later, she's on to something else. In the end, it's back to old habits and discouraging days. For Denise, it seems, there is nothing to do but cling to the brink of her sanity.

Meet Sondra, dwelling in peace just down the street. (Many of you met her in the preceding book in this series, *On Becoming Toddlerwise*.) She is not frazzled or fatigued and faces family dinnertime with creative enthusiasm. Baby Gregory is already sleeping through the night and taking naps like clockwork. As it is most days, two-year-old Katie plays contently with her doll house on a blanket in the family room while four-year-old Ben is trustworthy enough to play by himself in his room. If you drop in unexpectedly, you'll find the house picked up and Sondra will welcome you with a calm, warm smile. Are we still on planet earth?

A Tale of Two Mothers

You may recognize one of these moms, because one of these mothers most likely represents you. Denise and Sondra are not fictional characters, but real life moms in the thick of battle. Start with hampers of laundry awaiting your attention, trash cans on the verge of overflowing, and crumbs on the floor around the kitchen island that look more like boulders in need of excavation; then add in those little beings around the house with developing ideas, interests, and a whole slew of needs that seem new every morning—without a doubt, Mom is on the front lines every day. Of the two women described, both desire the same things in their parenting, marriage, and family. Yet Sondra has the clear advantage. She is not letting the rush of life manage her, but instead has learned how to mange life in her home with amazing results. What is it that Sondra knows? Simply this: Young children not only need, but they also crave supervision, direction, and encouragement. Random acts of parenting just aren't good enough to get through the day with one's sanity intact.

From an intellectual standpoint, everyone picking up this book would agree that young children need supervision. They are not mature enough to make wise decisions on their own or understand the dangers of running into the street. What supervision looks like in terms of everyday life, however, is often challenging for young moms.

Let's face it, children left unsupervised for great lengths of time are prone to get into trouble. Giving the dog a haircut, pushing buttons on Dad's cell phone, deciding it is snack time, or drawing on the bedroom wall all are snapshots of trouble. Without supervision, young children tend to choose how they will act based on what they want to do, not necessarily on what they ought to do or what is best for them. Supervision comes in the form of a person, not the television, and Mom is usually the one in charge. The most effective way to provide continual supervision for a preschooler and at the same time provide many opportunities for learning is by structuring your child's day.

In her book *Simplify Your Life with Kids*, Elaine St. James suggests, "Kids who live without structure can develop behavior problems. Frequent tantrums, whining, a disregard for rules, inappropriate or aggressive behavior, constant demands, and an inability to share are some of the signs that your child needs more structure."[6]

We concur with that assessment. To have routine, order, and structure is to think ahead and plan. Structuring your preschooler's day will eliminate a big chunk of stress on Mom because it reduces random opportunities for misbehavior. With thoughtful planning, Mom is proactive instead of reactive, meaning she can plan the day rather than react to each situation as it arises.

There are many benefits associated with a daily routine. Managing your preschooler's day enhances good organization, time-management skills, and provides an orderly environment for your children to optimize their learning experiences. It also helps Mom achieve personal and parenting goals while reducing the need for corrective discipline.

The Value of Routine

In the spring, ranchers typically check their fences and make repairs

---

[6]See Elaine St. James, *Simplify Your Life with Kids: 100 Ways to Make Family Life Easier and More Fun* (Kansas City, MO: Andrews McMeel, 2000), 172.

before the long grazing season begins. A consistent, reliable fence is critical to the welfare of the herd and the rancher's investment. Broken fences mean wandering livestock and loss of income. If the cattle broke through the fence only to stay close at hand (grazing just on the other side of the fence), letting them loose would not be a huge concern. However, the "other side of the fence" has neither the safety nor security of boundaries, and that is where the threat of potential danger and hazards awaits.

Parenting without some structure and routine in your day is like a rancher who lets his herd graze on the "other side of the fence." You have difficulty controlling situations because you do not know where your children are exactly or how far they have drifted from the boundaries of security. A daily routine provides safety zones in which your children can grow, learn, and play. It is a type of fence that can keep your child from getting into trouble or wandering off to forbidden zones—not just in a physical sense, but also in an emotional sense. A child who is not in frequent trouble does not need frequent discipline. Trying to correct a wandering child is like pulling back an angry cow using a shoestring. It is just too little, too late.

What Does a Routine Look Like?

Your preschooler's routine is both similar yet different from that of your toddler's routine. It is similar because there are three natural divisions in the day: morning, afternoon, and nighttime. Within each of these divisions are mealtimes and naptimes. The major differences between the two age groups are the types of structured play and learning times and the length of each activity. As Gary Ezzo and Dr. Bucknam shared in Chapter One, *Children Need to Play*, a preschooler's imaginative play takes up more time than a toddler's sense of curiosity. Therefore a preschooler's daily routine will have fewer activities than a toddler's, but longer periods of time at each event.

A return to some of the basic *On Becoming Toddlerwise* foundational tenets will help put your preschooler's routine on the right track. Consider the following:

Set Age-Appropriate Goals

In Appendix B of this book, *The Land of Good Reason*, Gary Ezzo and Dr. Bucknam write: "Parents need to refocus their thinking from how to handle a crisis to the heart of the matter—*Why* are they handling it?" They explain that the *hows* of parenting will result from the *whys* of parenting. *Why* we do what we do is the combination of our *beliefs* and our *goals* in parenting. What you believe about parenting will determine what goals you set for your children. Take a peek at that appendix. If your long-term goal is to raise a morally responsible and academically assertive child, than you may find it helpful. The following are examples of appropriate long-term goals parents set:

- Moral training—This category requires continuous education. Moral training develops your child's character through self-control, obedience, manners, patience, sitting, focusing, concentration skills, and relationships with peers, siblings, and adults.

- Academic skills—This requires the development of gross and fine motor coordination, ABCs, mathematics, language, reading, and more.

- Spiritual training—This relates to scriptural knowledge, memorization, catechism, or knowledge of historical characters of your faith.

Once you have set age-appropriate goals, devise a workable routine and structure your child's daytime to help achieve those goals. You might need to pay attention to one or several developmental concerns. These might include issues of aggressiveness, loudness, lack of eye contact, unwillingness to submit to your leadership, lack of age-appropriate self-control, or any one of a host of other educational, social, or emotional weaknesses evident in your child.

For example, Amy, our third child, entered her preschool years marked by a lack of staying power to focus on any one activity for longer than a few minutes (more like seconds!). It was a weakness we knew would be a problem in the future if she did not begin to establish the habits and skills of focusing, concentrating, and self-control—and soon! We put together our goal and devised our strategy. By the time Amy was ready to go to school, we wanted her to possess the self-control needed to sit, listen, and follow a task through to the end. To facilitate our goal, I set aside fifteen to twenty minutes each morning to work with Amy on "school." The purpose was not to teach her academics (we worked on that at other times), but specifically to work on her impulsive behavior.

An impulsive child is one who is always looking toward what is next rather than enjoying what is in front of her. This is a child who begins to color a picture, quickly grows impatient, begins to scribble the whole page, only to look toward starting over with another picture. If left uncorrected, this child becomes an unsettled adult, unable to stick with a single task very long without craving change. When forced to do a task, whether in the classroom or the workplace, he or she will fight boredom with mediocrity.

Uncontrolled impulsiveness spawns two developmental negatives: tasks poorly done, and tasks incompletely done. End result? A child who never achieves a personal sense of *accomplishment*, which is necessary to motivate a child to tackle bigger projects with confidence and pleasure rather than with fear and dread. Fear and dread are the resident emotions of children who routinely lack a fulfilled sense of accomplishment. They tend to get discouraged quickly and give up on tasks. We did not want this for our daughter nor did we want it to be the legacy of our parenting.

The process began by giving Amy a picture to color. Initially she would hurry through it, coloring excessively outside the lines and declaring "I'm all done!" I would remind Amy what I expected of her while handing her a copy of the same picture to color again. With the timer set, she had five minutes to color the picture correctly. If she finished ahead of time she had to sit quietly and patiently until the timer went off. If her picture was not neat (as neat as any four-year-old can make it), she received another copy of the same picture for another five minutes of coloring.

At first, Amy would go through six or seven pictures in a twenty-minute period of time. Once she realized that she wasn't allowed to get up or talk until the timer went off, she started to take her time coloring the picture carefully. Similar training spilled over to other venues, such as memorizing alphabet flash cards and working with matching games and puzzles that challenged her attentiveness.

There were wonderful conclusions from our efforts that year. At her first parent-teacher conference in kindergarten, we were greeted with a glowing report about our daughter's remarkable ability to sit, focus, concentrate, and patiently do her assigned work. More importantly, Amy began to achieve a sense of personal accomplishment by seeing a task through to the end, with excellence. This in turn gave her the confidence to face greater life challenges with success. No room was too messy to tidy-up, no school assignment too difficult to achieve, no hurdle too high to scale, no distance too far go.

Amy is now a teenager. As we look at her many accomplishments and awards received for music and character, we shudder to think what could have happened to her if we downplayed her impulsive behavior demonstrated in her preschool years. What if we declared the problem to be just a passing phase, or an unfixable quirk in her personality, or worse, labeled it hyperactivity? We recently watched a home video taken at Christmastime when Amy was four years of age. We all laughed, (including Amy) as we counted out loud the number of seconds before Amy moved, jumped, or bounced from one thing or person to another. We never counted more than five seconds. She was hyperactive! But it was fixable. Providing the fences of structure and routine was the right medicine for Amy. It allowed us to work on her impulsiveness without abandoning other priorities including her two older siblings, our friends, home, and marriage.

Writing out Your Routine

On a sheet of paper, write down all your daily activities, including what you need to do in a twenty-four hour period and what you would like to do beyond the normal and expected tasks. What about weekly and monthly activities? Consider your personal and family activities including housework, work schedule, shopping, children's activities, and the little details of life—such as haircuts, trips to the bank, changing the water in the fish tank, and vacuuming out the minivan. Don't forget your time away to get your nails done, meet a friend over a hot mocha, or meet Dad for lunch. Like most moms, you will probably be amazed at all the activities you manage to pull off in any given week. However, rather than falling into bed stressed and exhausted from just the thought of all that you do, give yourself a well-deserved pat on the back, sharpen your pencil, and let's get started on a management plan for your home, children, and day.

Once you consider the various elements that make your family unique, start sketching your plan. Take a second sheet of paper and divide it into half-hour or hour increments (or whatever time increments work for you). Start planning each day keeping in mind that the weekends are less structured than weekdays. There is a sample schedule at the end of this chapter to give you ideas to get you started. Use what you can of it. When looking at the example, please note the name that is missing. It's yours. Know that once you get your children's schedules under control, you will easily find time to manage the rest of your day.

The first slots that you fill in on your routine are meals and naptimes, as those should stay relatively constant. Next add the fixed activities that take place outside of the home such as Tuesday afternoon reading time at the library, Wednesday morning women's study at the church, and Thursday afternoon kinder-gym. Next, consider the general family needs—grocery shopping, a trip to the dry cleaner, carpool responsibilities, doctor and dentist visits—are all part of this list. Fit them in. Once those activities are written down, take a look at the rest of your day and start to fill your schedule in with your children's activities. There will be roomtime and playtime activities including painting, drawing, coloring, puzzles, and more. There is also school time, sit alone time, reading time with Mom, and some fun video time.

When You Are on a Routine, but Your Child Is Not

Before you proceed to the specific ideas and recommendations, let me SHOUT a warning to you. Your schedule is to serve you. You do not exist to serve your schedule. You must have flexibility built into your plans every day—no schedule is exempt from interruptions because life is filled with the unexpected. Your two-year-old has to go potty just when you sit down to read with your four-year-old. Moments later, the other child announces that the cat just threw up on the new bedspread. And in case you haven't noticed, household appliances always break at the worst time, lightbulbs burnout just before your guests are to arrive, and the local ant colony found your kitchen a refuge from two days of constant rain.

Some interruptions are just part of the course of life, and Mom has to adjust to the unexpected. However other interruptions are controllable. Yes, there will be times when one of your darlings decides it is a safe time to take advantage of a moment of confusion and venture someplace other than where he should be. Let's talk about how to handle this first, and then we will move to the specifics of your routine.

What and Where

Vocabulary is important to children. Specific words communicate specific concepts and expectations to children that otherwise would pass them by. In parenting, certain specific phrases have more meaning and get better responses than nonspecific communication. When a mother assigns a child to an activity, she is simultaneously establishing two facts: the *what* of his behavior and the *where* of his behavior.

What and *where* are the names of the fences that will keep your child out of trouble. *What* is the activity Mom decides her child will be doing, and *where* is the place Mom decides her child will do it. Whenever you observe your preschooler wandering away from *what* and *where* you have instructed him to be, pull him back in with the two questions: *"What are you supposed to be doing?"* (The child answers.) Mom asks next, *"Where are you supposed to be?"* (The child answers.) Unless there is an emergency to alter your plans, you can redirect your child back to the activity without much difficulty with just these two questions.

Getting the right answers from your child as to *what* he should be doing and *where* he should be is far better than Mom continually repeating her instructions, starting with the proverbial "I told you to…" The *what* and *where* questions will help your child take ownership of what is expected without constant reminders from Mom.

Morning Routine

As we begin to look at the specifics of what activities can be built into your preschooler's day, you will want to keep in mind the information you just read in Chapter Four, *The Choice Addiction*. In some of the activities that are listed below, Mom chooses *what* her child plays with and *where* he plays. When Mom chooses, she is building a fence around her active preschool-age child. The following are suggestions for a morning routine for preschoolers:

- You should set a consistent time for your preschooler to start his day. Most parents start between 7:00 and 8:00 a.m. You can start earlier or later, but whatever time you establish, stay consistent.

- The first rule for a happy child in the morning starts ten to twelve hours earlier. Do not let your child set his own bedtime. Mom and Dad, you need to decide when your child goes to bed. Do not keep him up late at night thinking he will sleep longer in the morning. Rarely does this work out and usually makes for a cranky child and a challenging day.

- You might consider establishing a fence around morning wake time. For the early years of the preschool phase, teach your child that when he wakes up in the morning (while he stays in bed), he calls out for Mom and Dad. He cannot get into trouble if he is not allowed to get out bed until you invite him to do so. For the child that wakes before Mom and Dad, you can place books by his bed and tell him that when he wakes up in the morning, he can quietly look at the books until Mommy or Daddy comes in to get him.

- Assist your children in getting dressed before breakfast. Three-year-old children are not completely capable of dressing themselves. You will eliminate many challenges in the morning if you choose what he is to wear and help him get started in the morning.

- Work with your child to put his pajamas away and straighten his bed. The preschool years are a great time to start teaching your child that it is his responsibility to take care of his things.

- Breakfast time.

- After breakfast start his morning routine.

ON BECOMING PRESCHOOLWISE

There are many activities that can take place. When determining how to structure your preschooler's morning, determine what activities fit your plan for the day. Again, we are providing you with suggestions. You do not need to do all that is listed, but some of the activities mentioned should be part of your child's day.

Roomtime—The practice of "roomtime" is not new to our *On Becoming Toddlerwise* audience. However, if this is all new to you, we have a few words of encouragement and caution. The purpose of roomtime is to teach your child to learn to play quietly by himself for an extended period of time. This helps him to learn to focus and play independently without having someone or something there to entertain him. If a child must always depend on others to keep him busy or entertain him, then his ability to focus and concentrate, which are necessary skills for life, is severely impaired.

In their book *Teaching Your Child Concentration*, authors Lee Hausner and Jeremy Schlosberg ask, "Why do we need concentration? Because our brains are limited. We can process only so much information at a single time. If we couldn't select and concentrate on one thing at a time, and stick with it long enough, we could never learn or even think. We must select and focus." They go on to say that concentration is essential to comprehending what is being read or heard; it is essential to the formation of memory, and the development of concentration is not automatic, but is a learned skill.[7]

---

[7]See Lee Hausner, Ph.D. and Jeremy Schlosberg, *Teaching Your Child Concentration* (Washington, D.C.: Lifeline Press, 1998), 24.

Select and Focus

During roomtime, select an activity for your child to do that will require him to focus and use his imagination, such as working with Duplo Blocks, Lincoln Logs, or Playmobile sets. This will teach him concentration. Your goal for roomtime for a preschool age child will be forty-five minutes. However, you will want to start with a much shorter increment of time, such as fifteen minutes. Set a timer for fifteen minutes. Setting a timer will reduce the annoyance of your child asking every few minutes, "When is roomtime over?"

Free Playtime—This is when your child chooses his activity. It is still supervised time because Mom is choosing what he does in this time slot, but it is free time because your child is making the decision on what to play with. For a preschooler, it might be playing with his sandbox and bulldozer in the backyard, or Lego time in his room.

Structured Playtime—This is different from roomtime in that it will not take place in the child's room but in some place determined by Mom. It might be playing with puzzles at the kitchen table, coloring, playing with the kitchen play center, etc.

Structured Playtime with Siblings—This activity can overlap with some of the others. For example, two siblings can be coloring at the kitchen table, playing in the backyard together, or sharing reading time. There will be many hours shared with a sibling, which is why we recommend some "alone" time for each child.

Playtime with Mommy—A time should be built into your daily routine for each child to receive individual time with Mommy, even if this is only fifteen to twenty minutes a day. Preschoolers love and need undivided attention from Mommy. Of course Mom can join her child in many of the above-mentioned activities throughout the day, but that may not always be possible for Mom. When children are busy with activities, Mom can turn her attention to household responsibilities.

Playtime with Friends—There is value in having time allotted during your week for your child to socialize with other children his age. If your child attends preschool, then his time there fills this need. Besides having a friend over, you might consider attending a story hour at the library or joining a small playgroup with like-minded friends.

Video Time—Instead of falling into the habit of putting on a video when the children become whiny and restless, learn to structure a video time when it works best for you. Look for a time of the day that is most stressful for you. For me, that was always when I was trying to get dinner ready. The videos used for three- to four-year-old children should be no longer than one hour in length, preferably one half hour.

As stated above, teaching your preschooler to focus and concentrate is a worthy goal of your parenting. Things that entertain, such as computer games, videos, and television do not accomplish this goal. The authors of *Teaching Your Child Concentration* explain it this way: "Because it jumps from image to image, television (and videos) neither encourages nor allows time for the viewing child to stop and

think about the ideas presented, or to inspire him to imagine or figure out the consequences of certain actions for himself. Before your
child has time to activate his own thinking and focusing processes,
there's another image on the screen, and then another."[8]

Afternoon Routine

The following are examples or what might be included in your afternoon routine:

- Lunch
- Naptime/Rest Time
- Roomtime
- Structured Playtime with Siblings
- Video Time

All preschool-age children need an afternoon nap or rest time.
The need for a nap or rest does not always mean a child will want to
take a nap. Again, this is the time for moms to remember their
goals—what a child wants is not always what a child may need. Too
often, Mom declares, "My little Becca gave up her nap when she was
two." No, Becca did not give up her nap; she simply won the battle.
You, the leader and manager of your child's activities, made a conscious decision to surrender. You, Mom, gave up the nap and all the
developmental blessings that go with it. You traded it in thinking it
would give you peace for that moment, when instead you created a
fatigued, cranky, not-so-happy child.

---

[8]See Lee Hausner, Ph.D. and Jeremy Schlosberg, *Teaching Your Child Concentration* (Washington, D.C.: Lifeline Press, 1998), 12, 13.

Do yourself, and your child, a favor by scheduling naptime into the day. Right after lunch is a typical time. Plan on your child taking a good two-hour sleep. Between lunch, cleaning up, and naptime, nearly three hours of your afternoon routine is already planned. Children need to have a consistent naptime! Some preschoolers need additional time to fully wake up from their nap, so for them you will want to plan a quiet activity to transition them back into their routine. This might be a good time for a juice snack and a short *Winnie the Pooh* video. Other preschoolers wake up full of energy and are ready to play in the backyard. For both types of wake-up moods, after naptime is a great time to run errands, go shopping, or visit a friend. You will do much better in a store with a well-rested child by your side than a tired one.

If there are school-age children in your family, your preschooler will be excited to see them when they get home. Provide sibling playtime or snack time together. Older children quickly learn that once they give younger siblings their undivided attention, that sibling is less likely to demand it from them (in a manner that will cause conflict) at a later time.

Transitioning from Naptime to Rest Time

When your preschooler starts to be awake through his scheduled naptime (around four years of age), then he no longer needs a nap *every* day. When this transition takes place greatly depends on the sleep needs of individual children.

Children don't suddenly one day stop napping forever. Everyone benefits when Mom sees it as a weaning process. When it is time for naptime/rest time, tell your child that he needs to lay quietly on his bed. He may have one or two books to look at during this time, but he must stay on his bed. Tell him that if he is sleepy, he should sleep, because his body is telling him he needs to sleep on that day. If he isn't sleepy, then he may look at the books. If he falls asleep, make sure you wake him at the normal time his nap would be over.

Suppose he looks at the books for forty-five minutes and then falls asleep. If you let him sleep for two hours, it may prove difficult to get him back into bed at his normal bedtime. This will cause a whole new set of problems, and you really do not want this to happen, as his body relies on that block of nighttime sleep. Wake him up from his nap at the scheduled time. (Knowing he will be cranky, do allow him to watch a video after you get him up.) Eventually, your child will nap on the days he needs to and rest on the other days. The transition from no naptime to rest time can take place over a period of six months to one year. You will find that your child will nap four to five times a week, then two to three times a week, until he gets to the point where he no longer needs a nap at all. On days he doesn't take a nap, if he gets cranky later in the day, you may want to put him to bed one half hour early.

If you have children who share a room and one is still napping and the other is transitioning out of naptime—put the child in transition in your room (or another quiet place where he is removed from the activity of the house) with a book or two.

Evening Routine

The evening routine usually involves another adult in the house—Dad! Every couple sets their own parameters when it comes to Dad and how immediately involved he becomes with the family after work. Some husbands jump right in and take over with the kids, and others need to unwind a bit from their day's work before they can focus on the family's needs.

What Can Be Included in the Evening Routine?

- **Dinner**—Mom can plan quiet playtime for the children as she is preparing the evening meal. If Dad is delayed or working longer than normal hours, Mom can feed the children rather than wait for Dad to come home. The longer young children have to wait for their meal, the more cranky they will get and the more difficult mealtime will be. Mom can eat with Dad when he gets home. Remember, evening activities should work towards quieting your children down and preparing them for bedtime.

- **Family Time**—This can include an activity that the entire family can participate in. Dad may read a book to the children or play puzzles or Chutes and Ladders. Save dessert for this time.

- **Dad's Time with Children**—Children need undivided time with their Dad, even if it is only a few minutes a day. Dad can spend time with one child while Mom is bathing the other children.

- **Couch Time**—As mentioned in Chapter Four, *The Choice Addiction*, it is important for children to see that their parents are getting along. They also need to understand that their parents have a relationship outside of their parenting. We have found that when a husband and wife sit on the couch for ten to fifteen minutes and talk with each other, it teaches the children that Mom and Dad are special to each other. This breeds security in children. Again, using a kitchen timer, start with five minutes and increase the time over a period of a couple weeks. Tell your children that this is Mommy and Daddy's special time for each other, and give them something special to play with during this time. Also tell your children that they should not interrupt Mommy and Daddy during this time. If Mom feeds the children before Dad gets home, then when Mom and Dad sit down to eat can work for couch time.

- **Bath Time**—While bath time is often playtime, there should be some limits. Decide how much time bath time is going to take. Allow your child to choose a couple toys to play with. Never leave a preschool-age child unsupervised in the bath.

Bedtime

In the song "Do-Re-Mi," Julie Andrews sings that the very beginning is the very best place to start. With reading you begin with A, B, C, but when structuring your child's day you must always start with the "Zzzzzzzzz's"! Sleep is the starting point of a very good day. How much sleep does your child get? Interestingly, what time a mom thinks her children go to bed and what time they actually get to bed can be two very different things. Try and keep track for one week the time your children are actually settled into bed for the night. Many a mom is surprised to find that it is a rare week that her children get to bed at the same time for three nights.

Preschool-age children need at least ten hours of sleep a night. Therefore, if your preschooler's day starts at 7:00 a.m., then he needs to be *in* bed by 7:30–8:00 p.m. each night. It is not uncommon for moms of preschoolers to think that when their children get to bed at 9:00–9:30 p.m. that this is "early." I often grocery shop late at night, and I am always surprised at the number of parents out with very young children. Typically, they are whiny and demanding, and the parents are usually threatening them in some way or another to get them to behave. It is unfair to expect over-tired young children to behave like well-rested ones.

When preschool-age children are not getting enough sleep, they are irritable, hard to manage, and have little or no self-control. Don't start your day with this child in your home! Getting your preschooler to bed by at least 7:30–8:00 p.m. each night will lessen the need for discipline and correction. Again, well-rested children behave better.

Did you know that children grow in their sleep? Around three to four years of age is a time of growth spurts in children. This is another reason to allot ten hours of sleep a night for your child. He needs it for optimum growth and health. Well-rested children do not get sick as often as children who are chronically over-tired.

If your child's bedtime is currently at 9:00 p.m. or later, begin to work toward your desired goal in fifteen-minute increments over the next few weeks. Put your child to bed at 8:45 p.m. for one week. Then move it to 8:30 p.m. the following week. Keep moving your child's bedtime up until he is waking up in the morning with a happy attitude. Don't start putting your child to bed at the time you decide is bedtime. Allow at least one half hour to get your child settled into bed. During this time you can say prayers and give final hugs and kisses for the night.

Helps for Establishing a Bedtime Routine

The following are guidelines that are helpful in establishing a bedtime routine.

- Set a time you can be consistent with.
- Avoid roughhousing and wrestling on the floor with Dad within a half hour of bedtime; it takes too much time for children to wind down.
- Avoid conflict prior to bedtime. This is not the time to get into power struggles with your child. Be directive in your instructions—instead of asking your child if he wants to get ready for bed, tell him that it is time to get ready for bed and go with him to the bedroom to get into his pajamas.
- Whenever possible, hire babysitters when you have to be out at night so your children's bedtime can be as consistent as possible.
- Avoid offering unlimited liquids after dinner. (It is not uncommon for preschool-age children to wet the bed. This will help with that.)
- Consider doing your story-time out on the couch or in your favorite easy chair and not in bed. This is a great time for Dad to be with the children. When story-time is over, off to bed they go. If you have story-time in the bedroom, you never finish because the child has no place else to go. "Off to bed" helps cure the habit of "read me another story."
- Experts on sleep disorders agree that it is best for young children to learn to fall asleep on their own. Give your child a favorite stuffed animal, kiss him goodnight, and quietly leave

the room. When starting this with your child, you may need to stay outside his bedroom door for a couple nights. If you hear him get out of bed, open the door and firmly instruct him to get back into bed. This can be hard on parents, but don't give in to pleas for more kisses and hugs, as this can be never-ending. After he figures out he can't get past the door, he will stay in bed.

- Have a rule that he may not get out of bed unless it is an emergency. Make sure he understands what an emergency is and what it is not.

- If your bedtime routine has been rushed or your child gets to bed late because of your schedule, you may want to consider playing soft music in his room to help him settle down.

Mealtime

America is raising too many obese children. Children load up on sugar, fat, salt, and caffeine every day. Please do not be misled. What your children eat will effect how they behave. If your children are chronically irritable, cranky, whiny, and unmanageable, the solution could be in their diet. This goes beyond looking at common food allergies. To get your child's diet under control, feed him at home. We encourage you to have regular mealtimes and healthy snacks. Fast food (including pizza) should be a treat, not a regular occurrence. Try offering soda as a special treat rather than an everyday part of a child's diet. If you are too busy to plan nutritious meals for your family, try using a Crock-Pot, and freeze meals ahead of time. It is well worth it.

Mealtime Guidelines

- Try to stay consistent with your mealtimes. Our bodies function best when we feed them at regular intervals.
- Serve your preschooler small increments of food. The current trend is to downsize portions. We give our preschoolers bigger portions than they need.
- Limit his drink while eating. Otherwise he will fill up on drink and not eat.
- Don't offer additional servings until he has finished what is on his plate.
- One of the reasons children are willing to make mealtime a battleground is because they are not hungry. If you are fighting with your child at mealtime, then limit the snacks and drinks he gets in between meals.
- Misbehavior during mealtime, such as messing around at the table, whining about the food served him, and slumping in the chair out of protest can best be handled by isolation. (See Chapter Eight, *Laws of Correction for Preschoolers*.) A chair in another room works effectively. Tell him that he can rejoin the family when he can behave and is ready to eat his meal. Your goal here is not to punish your child but to help him gain sufficient self-control to return to the table.
- Work on table manners early on. It is always appropriate to require your preschooler to say please when he wants something and thank you when he gets it.

When starting to think in terms of adding routine and structure to your day, start with the bedtime routine first, then work with mealtimes. You will be surprised at the difference in your children's behavior when they are well-rested and are eating nutritious meals on a regular basis. While making changes in these two areas might take a lot of work on your part, surely it is a better alternative than the other options: having to continually discipline irritable, misbehaving children or give them medication to settle them down. Once you have made progress in these areas, you can add routine in the rest of your day.

A Word to the Weary

We have provided numerous suggestions to help you establish your preschooler's routine. However, many reading this chapter may be feeling overwhelmed at this point. Begin slowly. Start with one thing at a time, like getting your children to bed at a consistent time at least five nights a week. When you see progress here, start on other parts of your day.

Some people chafe at the very notion of providing their children with structure. I was like that. I liked to "go with the flow," wherever the flow was going. But what that earned me were children who were argumentative, whiny, demanding, and not very well-behaved. I didn't care for the looks and whispers my children's behavior brought when we were in public. Like Denise, I was missing something and needed help.

When I was first introduced to the benefits of structuring my child's day, I found it hard to do. It meant I had to gain self-control in some areas of my life where I didn't want to admit I needed help.

But today, writing from the perspective of a mother with two teenage daughters and a son in college, I can speak of the wonderful benefits that came with structuring my day and that of my children. Structure and routine gave me the freedom to do many more activities with my children than I could when I had no routine. It will be the same for you.

It will not always be easy, because as moms we naturally wonder if our child is missing out on something. So we begin to add an activity here and another there. Before we know it, busyness controls our schedule. What I learned from my own experience is that preschoolers do not need to experience everything in their tender years of life. You do not need to sign them up for every music lesson, peewee soccer league, kinder-gym, or ballet class available for their age. They're wonderful activities, but your child does not need to experience them all. Too many away-from-home activities wear out child and mom.

If you ask parents of college students if they believe the activities they had their children involved in when they were toddlers and young preschoolers advanced them in any way, you will likely hear that they can't even remember them. Having your children in too many activities too early will burn them out emotionally and possibly neurologically. Pick one or two activities for your child to enjoy, and let the rest go. Simplify your life.

Whatever Happened to Denise?

Denise finally connected with her neighbor Sondra and learned the way of routine. She started setting a more conservative bedtime. Once that was established, she moved on to her daytime routine. Michael attended preschool two mornings a week. During one of these mornings Denise did her shopping and errands, and the other morning she took Kaitlin to story hour at the library. She even had time to enroll Kaitlin in a kinder-gym class. To Denise's pleasant surprise, the children did not complain about missing other activities. They didn't care. They were getting along better and even looked forward to the times Denise scheduled in their day for them to play together. It took time, planning, and perseverance, but in the end it was worth it all. Denise and her husband enjoyed having time alone in the evenings (now that the kids were in bed earlier), and their relationship was better for it.

Denise's schedule looked like this: Michael went to preschool on Tuesday and Thursday mornings from 9:30–11:30 a.m., and Kaitlin went to kinder-gym on Thursday morning too. That meant the Monday, Wednesday, and Friday schedule looked different from Tuesday and Thursday. Below is Denise's Monday, Wednesday, and Friday schedule. Take whatever you can use, and make your own schedule from it. Yours might contain more flexibility or be more detailed. Do what works for you. Try your schedule out, make adjustments, be flexible, and remember the first rule of routine—your schedule is to serve you and your child; you do not become a slave to the schedule. Finally, whatever you do, make sure you block out time for yourself.

Michael and Kaitlin's Schedules
Monday, Wednesday, Friday

  7:30 – 8:15 a.m. Get children up and dressed; PJs put away, beds made; enjoy breakfast
  8:15 – 9:30 a.m. Structured playtime with siblings
  9:30 – 10:00 a.m. Roomtime (Kaitlin); reading time with Mom (Michael)

10:00 – 10:30 a.m. Roomtime (Michael); reading time with Mom (Kaitlin)

10:30 – noon Free playtime with siblings (possibly one half hour of video time)

noon – 1:00 p.m. Lunch, clean-up, read books until naptime

1:00 – 3:00 p.m. Naptime (Kaitlin)

1:00 – 2:00 p.m. Rest time (Michael)

2:00 – 3:00 p.m. Free playtime (Michael)

3:00 – 4:30 p.m. Free playtime (Michael and Kaitlin)

4:30 – 5:00 p.m. Video time or structured playtime

5:00 – 5:30 p.m. Pick up house before Dad comes home

5:30 – 7:00 p.m. Dinner, Daddy, and family time

7:00 – 7:30 p.m. Time with Dad (Michael); Mom gets Kaitlin bathed and ready for bed

7:30 p.m. Kaitlin in bed

7:30 – 8:00 p.m. Michael gets ready for bed

8:00 p.m. Michael in bed

Chapter Six

Getting Ready for Kindergarten—Now

Robyn Vander Weide, Contributor

*I*t's the first day of kindergarten, and Mom is … where else? She's in her car enroute to school behind the big yellow school bus. So fitting. Standing self-consciously beside the safety of the swings, our nervous mom shifts back and forth anxiously awaiting the buzzer. She knows what every parent knows in their heart of hearts. Not only is this Suzy's first day; figuratively speaking it is judgment day for Mom and Dad.

Starting today, Mom and Dad will be graded on how well they prepared their child for school. Each family has made educational decisions (knowingly and unknowingly) during the preschool years that either set in place healthy learning patterns or will result in something short of acceptable. How do parents prepare for the former, the higher standard? The acceptable rather than reproachable? Can healthy learning patterns be served up like a plate of broccoli to assure academic fortitude? Or is readiness for school achieved through flash card training twenty minutes a day, or listening to language tapes? If only it was that easy!

The real secret to school readiness is much more basic, yet

broader in scope. Readiness skills are the by-product of decisions parents make during the preschool years of their child's life, not all of which are academic in nature. These decisions include how you view the importance of naps and nighttime sleep, types of activities children can be engaged in, proactive versus reactive styles of training, and the amount of structure and routine in a child's day. The decision parents make regarding these four activities sets in motion educational outcomes that are not easily changed in the future. For your child's sake, choose well your course of action. Let's start by looking at the importance of sleep for preschool-age children.

The Sleep Factor

Last night was a rough one. The dog was barking, and the electricity went out, causing phones to beep and bedside clocks to flash when some time later power was restored. Throughout the ordeal, you stayed horizontal. You don't specifically recall being really awake, although you're aware the outage occurred. The end result is a dead giveaway—this morning you are cranky, edgy, and wondering if an eighteen-wheeler drove across your bed looking for the highway. Simply put, you got a lousy night's sleep and every raw nerve ending on your body stands ready to proclaim it.

Now transfer this sleep quality to your child. When it comes to children, parents tend to think only in terms of two categories: their child is asleep or he is awake. In the book *On Becoming Babywise*, Gary Ezzo and Dr. Bucknam point out there is actually a gradation of sleep and wake times. Sleep ranges from a completely relaxed state, to active sleep, to groggy wake time, to complete wakefulness. Optimal wakefulness is directly tied to optimal sleep, and optimal development is directly tied to optimal wakefulness.

We cannot overemphasize that point. Preschoolers who suffer from the lack of healthy naps and nighttime sleep also experience a type of passive chronic fatigue, effecting maximum alertness. Who would want to live continuously in this condition? While a child may not suspect an off-course tractor trailer, nor even pinpoint the source of his agitation, the effect of too little sleep is equally devastating. It creates an alertness deficit, which further increases the child's inattentiveness while decreasing his focusing and concentrating skills. This child is easily distracted and often physically hyperactive. He is also more demanding, lacking the ability to interact within a learning environment for sustained periods of time.

In contrast, preschoolers who have established healthy sleep habits are optimally awake and optimally alert to interact with their environment. Having observed a generation of these children now, I see some common threads among the school-age population. In classroom settings, I have consistently found these children to be more self-assured, happier, less demanding, and more sociable, inspired, and motivated. They have longer attention spans and become faster learners because they are more adaptable. Mediocrity among this population is rare, while excellence is common.

In Chapter Two, *Factors of Learning*, Gary Ezzo and Dr. Bucknam make an important point regarding a child's ability to learn. They state that while parents cannot alter a child's intelligence quotient, they can maximize or limit it. One way this is done, both positively and negatively, is through sleep. The impact healthy and not-so-healthy sleep has on educational outcomes was first noted in a 1925 study conducted by Dr. Lewis M. Terman. Amazingly, his insights and conclusions related to factors influencing I.Q. continue to stand unchallenged to this day. His study looked at 2,700 children with superior intelligence and found one common link—all of them had experienced healthy nighttime sleep.[9] Good sleep habits are not a child's choice, but a parental decision.

Learning Activities

From handheld video games to dress-up trunks to harmonicas to markers, parents make decisions related to the activities they allow and provide for their children. There is little debate among educational clinicians that a child's ability to learn is tied to how the brain organizes information and what stimulates thought, ideas, and responses. This is one reason why a preschooler's imagination and play should not be hindered, but rather directed. Any activity that engages a child's interest, attention, or imagination fuels an active form of learning. *Active* is used here in contrast to the less desirable, passive form of learning, such as sitting too long and absorbing too many video or cartoon messages. These activities do not help with optimal brain organization because learning is passive and not interactive with a real person. It is one-way, stimulating the receptors but not allowing for interchange or response.

Trial and Error Versus Proactive Teaching

There once was a song about working your fingers to the bone, with the end result being simply, "What d'ya get? Bony fingers!" Likewise, let your young'un simply roam and what d'ya get? A roamin'

---

[9]Study cited in Marc Weisbluth, *Healthy Sleep Habits, Happy Child* (New York: Ballantine Books, 1987), 44.

young'un. There's no stick-to-itiveness behind the haphazard tasks your child approaches. This is another area impacting school readiness. Some educators suggest that the best way to teach children is to allow them to explore at will through trial and error discovery in an unstructured environment. No boundaries, no rules, no direction—only random discovery. The child learns only when the child is interested, and therein lies the problem. There is no back pressure to move the child to the next skill level necessary for future integration of lessons.

The trial and error theory supposes that parents should act only as facilitators of learning rather than as directors and teachers of knowledge. Allowing trial and error learning to become the primary source of education for your preschooler is risky and too often produces results that are far from satisfactory. It weakens a child's ability to assimilate new information with old knowledge previously acquired. As a result, the infrastructure aiding future learning fails the child. From this educator's perspective, one who now tests many of these children, I can only tell you trial and error discovery is not a good idea.

Structure and Routine

School readiness is greatly impacted by the orderliness of the home learning environment. In Chapter Five, *Structuring Your Preschooler's Day*, Carla Link did a wonderful job introducing the concept of structure and routine into your child's day. Establishing order and routine for your preschooler is not only less fatiguing for Mom, but has a profound influence on a child's learning abilities. Preschoolers flourish on consistency, predictability, and boundaries. When a child is at peace in his home environment, his learning potential increases and learning disorders are minimized. Having structure and routine in your child's day advances both of these causes.

On the first day of school, the child who possesses healthy learning patterns has parents who used the preschool years as a learning environment. These are parents who stimulated and guided their child's development, helping him gain useful information to grow in understanding and to attain important life skills. They knew how to strike a balance between these two extremes: On one end of the spectrum, the parent spends too much time with her child, not allowing certain skills of independence and focusing to develop; on the other end, the parent gives her child too much independence without enough instruction and routine to develop learning skills including expanding his attention span. A balanced approach to parenting a preschooler readies the child to be successful in school in all areas—including mental, physical, social, and emotional readiness.

The first step in a balanced approach to preschooler training is to develop a daily plan. The plan should include a combination of independent activities and activities with a parent, usually the child's mother. These activities will help develop general learning skills, specific learning skills, and necessary social skills needed for the child to be well prepared for attending school. The next step is to implement your plan. Here is what you need to know.

General Learning Skills

What kind of general learning skills does a child need to possess in order to be ready for school? The two bedrock skills necessary to build a firm foundation for learning include a strong attention span and the ability to focus. Each of these skills can be strengthened or weakened depending on how your preschooler spends his time during the day. The child whose parent provides structured learning is more mentally stimulated than the child who is given freedom of choice during his waking hours. This point is better understood in our next paragraph.

Attention Span

Jason says, "Candy Land." Mom says, "Okay." Jason says, "Find me!" Mom says, "Where is he?" Jason says, "Build blocks with me." Mom says, "What shall we build?" Jason says, "I don't want to build." So Mom, now confused, asks, "What DO you want to do?" Poor Jason; he really doesn't know!

If only Mom knew that a child's attention span develops best in a structured environment. This means a thoughtful parent determines the activities of the day, including the starting and stopping time of each activity, directed by Mom not Jason. Left to choose for himself, a preschooler will generally spend too much time flitting from one activity to another, or following Mom around expecting her to entertain him. Flitting and following generally lead to whining and discontent. Soon the child, like Jason, will be characterized as having a very short attention span.

As you develop a daily routine for your child, decide how long each activity will last. As your child grows and matures, work on increasing the length of time he spends happily engaged in each activity. This will increase your child's attention span.

Focusing Skills

Focusing is the ability to concentrate on an object or activity without being distracted by surrounding sights and sounds. Your child needs this ability in school so that he can complete an assignment in the face of distractions. In a school setting, these distractions can occur from the children around him, the decorations of the classroom, or noise from the playground. The ability to focus is developed in children by giving them time to play by themselves.

It is important for you to have a clear understanding of independent playtime in order for it to be an effective part of your child's daily routine. Let me explain what independent playtime is *not*. It is not time when your child chooses where to play, what to play with, and how long to play. (Remember our discussion in Chapter Five, *Structuring Your Preschooler's Day*, on building fences?) As we discussed on the previous page, a preschooler is not capable of making these decisions wisely. He will flit and follow and soon have a very short attention span.

Independent playtime begins early. By the time a child is between eighteen to twenty-four months of age, he should have developed the skill of learning how to spend forty-five minutes to one hour of uninterrupted time playing. Concentration and creativity are developed during independent play. The most important aspect of this time is that your child is learning to focus on what he can do with the things he has. This might involve playing with toys, puzzles, or books at an assigned time in an assigned place. To facilitate this goal, be sure that he is by himself, with no artificial forms of stimulation—meaning no computer games, Gameboys, or videos. Nor should he be in a place where he is easily distracted by watching you work or by listening to the vacuum cleaner or your conversation on the phone.

Keep his toys developmentally stimulating and challenging. One way this might be achieved is to rotate his toys. Children easily become bored when there is nothing new with which to play. Put some toys away for a few weeks or months, and then reintroduce them back into his play world. They will seem better than new because they are familiar old friends.

Specific Learning Skills

Flopping down a thirty-piece puzzle in front of your preschooler for the first time could be overwhelming for both of you. The question for him might well become, "How many of these knobby cardboard thingies can I smush in the cracks of my bedroom air vent?" Mom can do everyone a favor by spending time integrating each new skill at the various levels. Most specific learning skills will begin with this teaching time between parent and child. As the child learns the skill being taught, it can become an independent activity for him. Some specific examples are book time, puzzle time, and tape time. Each of these can become a twenty- to thirty-minute block of time in your child's daily routine. Let's examine the specific skills you should teach during the preschool years.

Getting Ready for Reading

It might be the wispy artistry of the illustrations, or the glossy bold cover design, or the weaving of the imaginary tale, or the oh-so-funny way the talking bear solves his problem. Whatever the reason, who doesn't remember that first magical moment when a book became something more than a book? It was truly a friend, the start of something new, or an opening to another time and place. Developing a love for books is foundational to becoming a good reader. To enhance this love, read to your child from the start. Books such as *Goodnight, Moon* and *The Runaway Bunny* are perennial favorites that preschool-age children enjoy listening to while being cuddled by Mom or Dad. On the question of book selection, it is all about variety. This could include heavy cardboard books for playtime or fun and silly stories for reading aloud. You also might read alphabet and rhyming books to develop phonemic awareness (sound/symbol relationships). As you build your child's library, be sure to include books about nature and the world around him. Most important are books that teach good character. Former Secretary of Education Dr. Bill Bennett compiled an excellent resource for character training. His *Book of Virtue* should be part of your personal library, and the stories contained within should find residence in the heart and mind of your child.[10]

Puzzles develop a child's ability to see how one part fits into the whole picture. This is not just fun and games, but a life skill perspective. Puzzles come in all different sizes, ranging from several pieces to several thousand pieces. They generally begin as a parent and child activity, but should quickly become part of your child's independent play. As a child's collection of puzzles grows, the pieces from two puzzles can be mixed. A sorting activity then takes place before the puzzles can be put together. Keep the puzzles challenging, but not so challenging that the child becomes overwhelmed.

Sequencing cards help children develop a sense of the beginning, middle, and end of a story. These cards can be purchased at an edu-

---

[10]Simon & Schuster, 1993.

cational supply store. They typically range from three-card sequences to six-card sequences.

Introducing children to the alphabet can begin with some kind of three-dimensional letters or alphabet cards. These can be made of plastic, sponge, or wood. Choose a "letter of the week," and point out all the things in your child's world that start with that letter. Initially you just want to help your child hear the beginning sound of a word. For example, you might say, "Yes, popcorn and peanuts both start with P." An alphabet book is very helpful. Choose one with lots of different pictures for each letter.

Getting Ready for Math

In the beginning, it's all about patterns. The child on the kitchen floor with the plastic stacking rings is learning the pattern *large to small*. For the preschooler, patterning activities include but are not limited to bead stringing, pegboards, and pattern blocks. When purchasing any of these items, be sure to include a set of patterns to be followed. These activities generally require plenty of parent involvement since preschoolers usually want to just play with the objects. With patience and repetition, children eventually learn to follow or reproduce the pattern, and the activity becomes much more rewarding than just free play.

Calendar activities are another good way to develop math awareness. A perpetual calendar works best—one in which the month, date, and day of the week are removable pieces. These can be found in craft stores, educational supply stores, or better yet, you can create your own. A very enjoyable morning routine develops when your child gets to place the pieces into the calendar and reviews the month, date, and day of the week. When the child is ready, it is easy to teach the concept of before and after. Let your child guess what the date is by looking at the number *before and after* the place for the current day's number.

Make counting a part of everyday life. Counting objects can take place anytime. Count fingers, toes, blocks, Cheerios, spoons, or just about anything. Counting out loud is a great activity for car rides.

Getting Ready for Penmanship

Getting ready to write is generally an activity for the child older than three years of age. In the beginning, writing and coloring have virtually nothing to do with lines and everything to do with *grip*. Because the thumb and pointer finger are uniquely wired to the brain, your child needs to learn to grip the pencil between the thumb and pointer finger, letting the pencil rest on the middle finger. The same grip should be used with crayons. It is very difficult for a classroom teacher to constantly check on each student's pencil grip. Therefore this skill is best taught at home.

Help your child use *relaxed* rather than cramped movements as he learns to color and write. Later you will teach the importance of staying in the lines or on the line. But in the beginning, correct grip and relaxed movement should be encouraged and praised.

Tracing offers your child many different opportunities to practice correct pencil grip and to strengthen the muscles of the hand. The easiest stencils to trace are the frame type, where the child traces around the inside of the shape. Later your child can progress to shaped stencils, which must be held in the center while tracing around them. Placing tracing paper over simple coloring book pictures offers another opportunity to practice good pencil grip. Children love the great pictures they can "draw" by tracing.

Cutting also helps develop the muscles of the hand. We use the same fingers for gripping the pencil and holding the scissors. Parents can teach cutting skills by using one-inch by six-inch strips of construction paper. With a felt pen, draw vertical lines about one inch apart on the strip of construction paper. Give the paper to your child to cut. When your child can hold the scissors properly and successfully cut on the lines, draw diagonal lines for your child to cut. Then progress to curved lines. Repeat this process with two-inch and three-inch strips of paper.

Getting Ready for Art

You can call it craft time, cut and paste time, fun time with Mommy, or making a prize for Daddy. No matter what you call it, know that time spent introducing your child to various types of art media impacts his attitude about art. Preparing your child to enjoy art involves both art skills and art appreciation. Art appreciation in this context does not involve visiting a museum or evaluating paintings— wondering what an artist was attempting to communicate. We are using the term here in a generic and practical sense, with an emphasis on learning shapes, sizes, colors, and patterns. Beginning art skills include cutting, coloring, and learning to draw simple geometric shapes, such as circles, squares, and triangles. These activities require a certain amount of fine motor development that is not usually present until about three years of age. However, art appreciation can be taught as soon as the child can match like items and put together simple puzzles. Parents can purchase or easily make color cards to teach children to match like colors. This activity becomes more difficult when varying shades of each color are introduced.

A wonderful way for parents to teach children to recognize and appreciate great works of art is to make puzzles out of copies of the artwork. After the copy has been laminated, cut it into five or six pieces for your child to reassemble. As the child grows, the picture can be cut into smaller pieces to increase the difficulty. Museum bookstores have poster-sized art reproductions that can make great floor puzzles. It helps if you also purchase a postcard of the artwork for your child to look at as he puts the puzzle together. Keep an eye out for used books that contain pictures of great masterpieces.

Getting Ready for Music

Children should be introduced to music ASAB (as soon as birth!) or sooner. Keep a small CD or tape player handy in your child's room. Classical music is a good place to begin. You may be thinking, "I don't really know classical music, and I'm not sure I will like it." In reality, you are probably familiar with classical music more than you are aware. Familiar themes are used quite often in movies and advertising. Find several CDs or tapes you like, and play them as background music during your child's playtime. Classical music is unlike other forms of music. It provides excellent auditory stimulation for the brain as it has definite, orderly, mathematical patterns.

Your preschooler's music library should grow to have lots of variety. You can include tapes of patriotic songs recorded especially for children to help develop appreciation for our country and pride in being an American. Folk songs are an easy way to begin learning about different people and times in our country's history. You may choose to use Sunday school songs that will teach your child about good character and the love of God. Your educational supply store or local bookstore will carry these tapes and may also have tapes that use music to teach other academic concepts. Stock up, because music is such an enjoyable way to learn, and it is good for the soul.

Encourage your child to sing along with the tapes. Your child's listening skills will grow if you teach him to sing on pitch. For some children, learning to sing on pitch is difficult and takes time. Always be positive and encouraging. Otherwise your child may decide that singing is hard and clam up. Make sure singing is always fun.

Rhythm clapping is an excellent way to develop listening skills (in this case, auditory sequential memory). Here is how this works. Clap a simple rhythm pattern and have your child mimic it. As your child's listening skills grow, the patterns can become more difficult. This activity can be enjoyed just about anywhere, although sometimes you may need to clap quietly.

Getting Ready for History

If it didn't really happen, let your child know. That makes the events that really, really did occur mean all that much more. Did Jackie Robinson really get jeered by the crowd? How did he respond? Did Helen Keller's ears and eyes not work at all? How was she able to overcome those odds? Children thrive on these lessons of life. Stories like these encourage your child to enjoy history and take an interest in it. Give your child plenty of opportunities to listen to stories about the lives of real people. These stories can be read from books or listened to on tape. Be on the lookout for short, simple picture books and audiotapes that tell the story of historical characters. Story tapes are a good quiet time activity and are useful in the car. Topics for beginning history books include the story of the Pilgrims and the first Thanksgiving, or the charity of the Patron Saint Nicholas and the Christmas story. There are also some excellent videotapes that should be used in addition to, but not in place of, books and audiotapes.

Getting Ready for Science

Take the morning after a rain, a quiet street, and motionless worms scattered upon it, and you've got the makings for science. Yukky? Yes, and all the better! Why are they here? Where are they going? What do they feel like? How do they move? Preschool science can be summed up in three words: observation, conversation, and exploration. Science is all around us, so teach your child to be an observer. Observe the growing process in your own backyard. You may even want to plant some seeds, water them, and watch them grow. Observe insects, animals, the weather—whatever science is going on around you. This observation should naturally lead to conversation.

Talk to your child about the world in which he lives. These conversations will give him needed information and increase his vocabulary. You can use very simple words to explain what happens when we plant a seed in soil, water it, and expose it to sunlight. Do not become obsessive and feel that you must explain everything to your child. However, do not miss natural opportunities to talk to him about his environment.

The observation and conversation can be greatly enhanced by exploration into simple books, videos, and games about science. A basic video discussing the process of how the body heals a cut can have your preschooler expounding on white blood cells, platelets, and fibrins in no time at all. This is good not just for impressing your mother-in-law; your child may actually come to understand some complex workings of the human body. At the very least, he comes away with a greater appreciation for the workings of living things.

Libraries and bookstores have beautifully illustrated picture books about animals, the seashore, the woods, and many other science topics. Most libraries also have videos of nature and animals available to loan. Educational supply stores and catalogues carry colorful puzzles and simple matching games about animals and ocean life. The key is to keep it simple and on your child's level. Remember, you are just laying the foundation.

Social Skills

The final element of school readiness is social. A child who comes to school with an understanding of how to behave in a classroom setting is more likely to have a positive first impression of school than the child who is unfamiliar with classroom and playground procedures. With a little bit of explanation and practice beforehand, your child can be ready and even excited about starting school.

Getting Ready for the Teacher

For a number of years I taught a kindergarten class for four-year-old children. I expected to spend the first week of school teaching the children classroom habits and procedures. The transition to school was easiest for the children whose parents had already taught them appropriate school behavior. Certainly a good teacher will explain all of this to the students, but children will feel so much more confident if they know what to expect and what will be expected of them. An experienced teacher always appreciates the child who just seems to know what to do, and the inexperienced teacher finds the prepared child to be a godsend. Some of the behaviors you will want to teach include:

- Standing and walking in line
- Raising your hand and waiting to be called on
- Listening to the teacher and following directions
- Not talking or whispering to other students while the teacher is talking
- Not talking or whispering to other students while children are working quietly at their desks.

You can easily teach your child these behaviors by explaining the correct behavior and following up with a fun time of practicing the behavior. For instance, you can teach that when the signal is given to get in a line, you should walk to the designated spot and stand *behind* anyone who is already in line. Stand with your face forward and your hands at your side. Keeping your face forward while walking in line is important. If you turn around and look behind you, you will not know when the line stops moving until you run into the person in front of you.

Next you can give your child an opportunity to practice lining up. You can have fun laughing together as you demonstrate what *not* to do. This could include pushing into the middle of the line or insisting on being first when others are already in line. Assure your child that while he will not always get to be first, he will eventually get a turn to go first.

Explain to your child that one of the problems in a classroom is what to do when several people want to talk at the same time. This problem is solved when a child raises his hand and waits until the teacher calls his name before speaking out. In Chapter Two, *Factors of Learning*, Gary Ezzo and Dr. Bucknam discussed the *interrupt courtesy*. Teaching your preschool-age child to use his hand to interrupt Mom and Dad when they are conversing with someone or talking on the phone will enable him to easily grasp the concept of raising his hand and waiting for the teacher to call on him once he starts school.

It is important to teach your child to listen to the teacher when she is talking so that he will know what to do. You could tell him, "We talk to our friends *during playtime*; we *listen carefully* when the teacher is talking." Help your child be a good listener by teaching him how to stop talking. Children who never learn this skill are hampered academically, and teachers find them irritating. If your child loves to talk, practice riding in the car with no talking for five minutes. For the talkative child, silence can be quite a challenge. Have your child tell you what he saw out the window during the quiet time. Silence is a valuable self-discipline and usually heightens a child's powers of observation.

As an alternative to talking, you might play the game "What Does Mommy See?" Start with one-minute increments and work your way up to five minutes, or start with half-mile increments and work up to two miles. The purpose is to help your child learn to focus, identify, and retain. You can work with colors, sizes (tall, short, round, or thin), patterns, or almost anything else you think is important. For example, pick several large items on the roadside, such as the big barn, the bridge, the school bus, and the water tower. After a minute, ask your child, "What did Mommy see that was big?" The child's job is to learn to recognize and file away in his memory possible answers. Next move to colors. "Mommy is going to look for the color red." Go a mile and ask your preschooler what he saw that was red. This little game is a wonderful substitute for aimless talking, and it increases your little talker's focusing abilities at the same time.

Getting Ready for Social Interaction

Getting ready for school also includes knowing how to make friends. This is not something children automatically know how to do. Good social skills should be taught and practiced over a period of time. Talk about things to say as "icebreakers" and how to show interest in the other person. Introduce the concept of what it means to be a friend and how being a friend leads to *having* a friend.

When my children were young, I looked for friends I trusted who had children the same age as mine. We would have exchange play days. One week the children would play at my house. The next week they played at the second home and so on. Also stay mindful of the importance of group play and activity versus a twosome activity. Your child needs to experience playing with a peer at some times and with a peer group at other times. The dynamics of playing with one friend and playing with multiple friends are different, and a child must learn to experience both.

In order for this to be successful in our exchange play days, some careful planning was required. I developed a simple plan for the playtime that included time to look at books, listen to tapes, watch a short video, as well as time to play with toys. I talked to my child ahead of time about what activities the children could do together. On the play date, I welcomed the friend to our home, helped the children get started playing together, and then watched or listened from the next room. During this time I learned which social skills my child had learned and which needed some more instruction and practice. I tried to leave the children alone as much as possible, giving them a chance to decide together what to play and to work out for themselves any problems that developed. Usually after forty-five minutes or so the children were ready for an activity that I would direct, such as book time or tape time. Snack time was always a hit. This might be followed by a second playtime.

Here are some things to watch for during the play date:

- How well does my child share?
- Is my child bossy, or does he speak kindly to the other child?
- Did my child insist on choosing what to play, or did he let the other child choose?
- How well did my child obey me in front of the other child?

The answer to these questions will give you an indication of your child's ability to play well with others.

After the play date, you should talk to your child. Find out what he enjoyed doing and what he thought was hard to do. Tell him what he did well. Be sure to praise specific times when your child talked kindly, shared, and obeyed. Point out the behaviors that were not appropriate. As you talk about the correct behaviors, it may be helpful to role-play so that your child can practice doing the right thing.

Getting Ready for Mom as Teacher

For those of you who are contemplating homeschooling, here are several things to consider. First, while your child may not need to raise his hand or stand in line, there are other social settings where those behaviors are necessary. Therefore, you should still teach these skills and even practice them occasionally.

Second, if you are already homeschooling older siblings, you will find it very helpful to have your preschooler on a routine that is developing productive independence in many areas. As you organize your homeschooling day, the activities explained in this chapter can become "schooltime" for your preschooler.

Third, pursue excellence. Give your child the finest education you can by choosing academically sound curriculum with a track record of producing competency in the students who use it. Talk with homeschool parents with children older than yours about what options are available and what they have found beneficial.

Fourth, plan the work and work the plan. Be careful not to scrimp on teacher materials and curriculum guides. These will help you develop a plan for the year, the quarter, the month, and the week. Once you have made the plan, stick with it. Develop good daily work habits. Play days and field trips are beneficial activities, but routine progress toward your goals is necessary in order to attain excellence.

Finally, remember your priorities. You are a wife and mother first. The benefits of homeschooling should not come at the sacrifice of quality family relationships, or at the sacrifice of your health and well-being.

Summary

Parenting is an ongoing process of preparing your child for the next phase of life. It is true that you cannot absolutely guarantee your child's success in school. However, there is so much you can do to help your child develop a thoughtful and inquisitive mind, a genuine love of learning, and the habits to be a good student. Yes, it takes effort to plan and effectively teach your preschooler. But the rewards for you and your child will pay dividends for a lifetime.

Chapter Seven

Developmental Placement–A Key to School Success

Robyn Vander Weide, Contributor

*Y*ou've paid your dues. From teething to T-ball and zippers to phonics, you've covered all the bases. You've invested five years in getting the little guy up to speed socially and academically. Now you're on the home stretch. He's turning five this summer, and boy, are you ready to sign him up for school. Without a doubt you are ready, but is he?

The education of your child from kindergarten to high school graduation is a thirteen-year marathon. Successful endings are very much tied to successful beginnings, which for children start during the preschool years when parents are shaping habits of the mind and heart. In our last chapter we discussed how to get your child ready for school, what general and specific skills to work on, and how to prepare your child for reading, writing, and arithmetic. This chapter primarily addresses a weighty and often misunderstood subject affecting your child's academic success—*developmental placement*. This is a key to school success and an important subject for parents to understand.

Simply put, developmental placement assumes a child has the greatest chance for success in school if he begins when he is developmentally ready. This means that starting formalized school, such as kindergarten, should be based on a child's developmental age rather than his chronological age. Educators who adopt this philosophy believe that children should begin school, or be placed in a particular grade, not by their birth date, but by an evaluation of their mental, social, emotional, and physical ages. Taking this approach up front can save everyone a more difficult situation later.

Dr. Arnold Gessell, an educational researcher from the early twentieth century, studied children from birth through sixteen years of age. He compiled lists of average behavior at each six-month interval. Today, educators continue to use Dr. Gessell's observations to help evaluate a child's rate of development. This evaluation, or developmental testing, often takes places prior to entrance to kindergarten.

During developmental testing, a child is given a series of tasks. A trained evaluator observes how a child approaches and completes the tasks. The evaluator can then determine if a child's developmental age is similar to a child's chronological age, a little older than his chronological age, or a little younger than his chronological age.

The Why of Developmental Placement

Chloe is reading simple words, yet she looks down and turns away if another child approaches. Jason is everyone's buddy at the playground, but a simple game of match reveals he couldn't find a pair of turtles if they poked their heads out from under the squares. Just as each child is unique, so is each child's rate of development. Some children develop more rapidly, others at a slower pace. Rate of development is different than mental ability. You may have a child of average to above average mental ability whose rate of development is similar to his chronological age, faster than his chronological age, or slower than his chronological age. Proper developmental placement will offer the following benefits:

Offers Greatest Opportunity to Reach Potential

We've all imaged that Kodak moment when, pigtails flapping in the breeze, our little sweetheart flings herself off the big yellow bus and dashes up the drive with a Rembrandt-like masterpiece draped over her arm and a pointy heart-covered pencil pressed oh-so-grownup down on her ear to declare, "School is simply the best, Mom!" *Snap*. That moment is more likely yours when the child is developmentally ready for kindergarten. Then, and only then, is she able to get the most out of the educational experience.

Such children understand what the teacher is teaching. They find the assignments challenging and enjoyable. Learning is exhilarating. They feel smart! When children are not ready for the academics of kindergarten, they feel frustrated by the teaching. They think school is boring and the activities are too hard and not worthy of their effort or time. They would rather be outside playing. Schoolwork does not make them feel smart; often it is quite the opposite. They tend to compensate for what they perceive to be a lack of smart thinking with naughty behavior, acting out in class to offset their perceived identity. Any child would rather be known as class clown than class dummy.

Developmental placement helps to optimize a child's educational experience. If the class clown above were properly placed (meaning starting school a year later), he would more likely have been at the top of the class, enjoying his learning experience and forming a completely different and wonderfully positive classroom identity that would see him through the next twelve years. The point? What a difference a year can make.

Limits Learning Difficulties

You only get one chance to make a first impression, so the saying goes. So it is with school. A child's first experience with school can leave an impression that lasts for an academic lifetime. Some have estimated that as many as 50 percent of learning difficulties can be eliminated through proper developmental placement. Let me explain. It appears that some children develop mental processing difficulties when they are placed in academic environments that require skills they have not yet developed. Other children develop learning difficulties when the pace of the curriculum is too fast for them to thoroughly process. They have trouble learning the new concept being taught because they have not yet fully mastered the previous concept. These children feel constantly bombarded with new information that does not get properly stored in their memory and then cannot be remembered when needed.

But this is nothing new to an *On Becoming Babywise, Toddlerwise,* and *Preschoolwise* audience. Gary Ezzo and Dr. Bucknam have repeatedly advised parents of this developmental fact. In *On Becoming Babywise II* they wrote: "Children interpret new experiences in relationship to knowledge formerly acquired. That means learning is progressive, and a child only gains understanding when new information has meaning in relationship to previous experiences. Routine and orderly transition at each stage of the child's development aid the marriage between new information and a child's understanding."[11]

In all my twenty-five years of education service as a teacher and school principal, I have never come across classroom evidence that runs contrary to that developmental truth above. Not only does preschool training establish right or wrong learning patterns; those very learning patterns ultimately influence developmental placement and your child's future.

School Is Appropriately Stressful

In an adult's busy world, stress is usually perceived as negative. Actually, stress can have either a positive or negative effect. Consider any stringed instrument. It is the stress on the string that produces the beautiful sound. The key, though, is appropriate stress. If the string is too tight, the note will be sharp. If it is too loose, the note will be flat. School should be appropriately stressful. If children are developmentally ready for the concepts being taught and the work being assigned, the stress is stimulating and future scholars are nurtured. If a child is not developmentally ready, the stress can be too much. School becomes frustrating and learning is stifled. I can say with confidence that the parents who bathe themselves in the principles of *On Becoming Babywise*, *On Becoming Babywise II*, *On Becoming Toddlerwise*, and *On Becoming Preschoolwise* will have children that enter school already ahead of the curve. Stay with it.

---

[11] See Gary Ezzo and Robert Bucknam, *On Becoming Babywise II* (Parent-Wise Solutions, 2001), 26.

Time for Extracurricular Activities

When a child starts school before he is developmentally ready, he may have difficulty understanding and completing the work assigned. If this continues for any length of time, the child falls behind. Also, many schools send home packets of simple assignments for the students to complete and return. Yes, even kindergarteners may have homework. If the student did not learn the concept in school, what should be a simple assignment can become a nightmare for both parent and child, and as a result, completing homework takes far more time than the teacher intended. As this pattern continues, the child does not have time for after school sports or music lessons. All extra time is devoted to schoolwork.

At this point, the joy in learning is zapped, and any additional activities that require effort, practice, and mental exertion are way low on the child's want-to-do list. There's simply nothing left for spontaneous interests. For these floundering souls, the television is a tempting soother, requiring nothing in return.

The When of Developmental Placement

In general, parents first think about their child's developmental placement prior to his starting kindergarten. Many schools schedule a developmental evaluation in late winter or early spring for all students planning on attending kindergarten in the fall of that year. A thorough developmental evaluation should take about forty-five minutes. The information gathered during this time will not only indicate readiness for kindergarten, but it is also a good predictor of readiness for the continuing years of elementary school. Although children have developmental growth spurts and plateaus, it is generally accepted that if your child is developmentally four years old at the time of testing, he will most likely be developmentally five years old a year from the testing date.

However, if a child demonstrates that he is not yet ready for kindergarten, there are several options. Some schools offer a two-year kindergarten program. Other parents choose a year of preschool or to keep the child at home one more year. This should not be considered as an affront to your child's intelligence, but rather a strategy to help your child maximize his intellectual abilities.

Who Are the Children in Need of an Extra Year?

Those working with developmental placement take into consideration certain facts of a child's life when making an assessment. These factors include:

Later Birthdays

Children born in the second half of the year (late spring through fall) may benefit by waiting a year before starting kindergarten. This is especially true of boys. Experience has shown that you can draw a line between June and July. Most boys born before July are ready for kindergarten as five-year-olds. Most boys born after June do better if they enter kindergarten as six-year-olds. For girls with birthdays in July and August, some are ready, but many are not. And even though a few states allow it, virtually no one turning five years of age after September 1 should start school until the following year.

Physical Challenges

Physical challenges that affect children's rate of development generally fall into two categories: premature birth and extended illness. Here are the reasons.

The rates of development inside the womb and outside the womb differ greatly. Babies inside the womb develop at a greater accelerated speed than outside. After birth, the rate of development slows dramatically. If a baby continued to develop after birth at the same rate as in the womb, the average size of a one-year-old would be one hundred pounds. Consequently, when a child is born prematurely, development that would have taken place in the womb is now taking place outside the womb at a much slower pace. That can and often does have an impact five years later, when the child is chronologically ready for school.

Because the child was not full-term at birth, the birth date does not accurately represent the child's age developmentally. If this child's birthday is close to the cutoff date for kindergarten, it is generally best to give him an extra year before starting kindergarten to ensure that all areas of development are strong. When it comes to testing a child born prematurely, as a general rule of thumb, I subtract one month from his current age for every week he was premature. For example, when testing a four-year-old who was three weeks premature, it is not uncommon to find a developmental lag of three months behind children of his same chronological age. Here I must emphasize to the reader that this has nothing to do with the child's intelligence, but with how to best optimize a child's intelligence and learning experience.

Similarly, children who have an extended illness or repeated hospitalizations during the early years of life usually experience some slowing in development while their bodies deal with the physical stress of illness and healing. This may explain why some of their behavior seems younger than their chronological age.

Emotional Challenges

As was previously mentioned, children's development takes place in four main areas: physical, mental, emotional, and social. Unusual stress in one area may slow development in other areas. This does not mean that stress alters the I.Q. or the ability to reach potential. Rather, for a period of time the mind changes focus from normal stimulation and development to preoccupation with the stressful situation. This is especially true of children experiencing divorce or the death of someone to whom they were close. This may cause a child's rate of development to slow down and therefore should be considered when determining developmental readiness for kindergarten.

Social Challenges

Making friends or adjusting to new situations can be very difficult for some children. While a child may be ready for the academic work of school, he may not be ready for the social setting found in the classroom. Giving him a year to mature socially may make the difference between a scholar with a well-rounded personality and a child who excels academically but has no idea how to make and keep friends.

Slower Development

Some children just develop more slowly. It's as if the developmental clock that is ticking inside them is just running at a slower pace than other children's. Rather than be frustrated by this, a wise parent will give this child the time needed to fully mature and won't try to rush things in order to keep pace with others. If this is your child, give him the gift of time needed. He *will* reach his full potential.

The How of Developmental Testing

Since the 1950s, a variety of tests have been developed to determine children's developmental age. Many private schools use these tests to determine readiness for kindergarten. The test measures development in several areas. The first area is adaptive behavior. How well can a child look at a model and reproduce it? The model may be three-dimensional (such as blocks) or two-dimensional (such as copying geometric shapes or completing a drawing of a person).

Another area that is measured is language development. Some of the activities may include answering simple questions, following simple directions, identifying items in pictures, repeating a series of numbers, and recognizing letters and numbers.

It is also important to evaluate children's gross and fine motor skills. A child's physical development is related to his readiness to read. Can he balance on one foot, hop on one foot, throw and catch a beanbag? Also, how well does a child handle a pencil or build with blocks? Does the child do these things in a way that is like the average four-, four-and-a-half-, or five-year-old?

The evaluator giving the test has a number of materials that help her accurately determine a child's developmental age in each of the areas tested. She also is able to gather information and make observations about your child's social and emotional development. All of this information helps the school and the parents make wise choices about when a child is ready to start kindergarten.

How Can I Prepare My Child for a Developmental Test?

The answer to this question is *"Don't!"* You should prepare your child for school, but not for a developmental test. A developmental evaluation is not a test that your child will pass or fail. It is an opportunity to gain valuable information about your child's rate of development and how he responds in that type of situation. Yes, you may feel nervous and want your child to do everything perfectly. But you need to remind yourself that you are only at the beginning of the long road of formal education. You need to look at the facts regarding your child's development rather than pushing him to a readiness level by performing on a test that will not be reflective of how well he performs in a classroom. Remember, your goal is for your child to enjoy school and be able to achieve his full potential.

A developmental test is a very special opportunity to take a peek inside your child's life. You get to watch how he thinks, solves problems, and responds to a variety of tasks. If you train him to do these tasks for the test, you will not have increased development, merely taught an activity. Also, you will have missed out on a wonderful opportunity to get some valuable information about your child's rate of development.

Let me share a personal example. I began giving developmental tests about five years before my children were born. By the time my first child arrived, I had tested several hundred children. I had seen what a special time this was for both parents and children. For about forty minutes (the length of the test), parents watched their child answer questions and perform tasks. Some of the tasks were familiar; some were not. Parents saw whether their child was calm or nervous, quiet or talkative, passive or active. Parents learned how their child related to the evaluator and how dependent their child was on the parents to help with or approve of the work completed. All of this is important information in assessing a child's rate of development.

After I became a parent, I knew that when my child was approaching kindergarten age, I wanted the same opportunity. I wanted to observe my child taking a developmental test. I knew the value of the testing situation, and I didn't want to skew it in any way. I never talked to my children about what was on the test, or let them touch or play with any of the testing materials. Consequently, my husband and I enjoyed very informative testing situations with each of our children.

Covering Some Basics of Successful Education

Looking back at when that first little infant was placed in your arms, who would have dreamed that getting him educated would be a major ordeal? It seemed simple enough—put him on the big yellow bus to school, where he spends several hours a day, until the little guy wiggles back in the door with a head full of ABC's and a snack time tale about Bobby's cracker creation. Yet somewhere along the line, it gets complicated because suddenly you realize that there's quite a bit at stake here. As a result, a little bit of panic sets in.

We've discussed at length how to prepare your child for school and how to make sure he starts school when he is truly ready. These chapters on education would not be complete without some focus on you and your perspectives on education. Or, more accurately put, keeping your child's education *in perspective*. The principles that follow may seem very basic, and that's because they are. They are common-sense reminders that should help you stay focused on the main thing—raising a morally responsible and academically assertive child who will successfully integrate his life into society for the benefit of all. Let's get started with our first educational truism.

There Isn't One Choice That Is Best or Right for Everyone

This applies to almost every aspect of education. For instance: public school, private school, religious school, homeschool? Each has merit, and one will fit your situation better than the others. You may not make the same choice as other relatives or friends. That doesn't make the choice right or wrong, good or bad. Make your choices based on your child's needs and what venue of learning can best facilitate your family and parenting goals. Fallacious is the reasoning that says there is only one way or place for a child to be educated. Don't be swayed by peer pressure, because what may be good for your neighbor's child may not be good for you. Also, if you are not sure how to make the best decision, become thoroughly acquainted with Appendix B, *The Land of Good Reason*. This narrative is a tremendously helpful tool that will show you how to crystallize your beliefs, set your goals, and create strategies to help you achieve those goals, especially in regards to the education of your child.

When it comes to selecting the best choice in education, the first consideration on the minds of many parents today is the *health* and *safety* factor. Because of the tragedies over the last decade in several of America's public schools, many parents are considering private schools as an alternative venue for educating their children. But private schools can be expensive, and they're not right for every child or family. If your child goes to a private school, he may have to forgo extracurricular activities, including organized sports, band, or choir that are common in public schools. On the other hand, the student-to-teacher ratios are usually better at private schools, and teachers can give more attention to character training and less attention to political correctness in the classroom.

Homeschooling is another option to consider. This movement, once popular primarily among Evangelical Christians, has now become quite fashionable in the mainstream culture. However, as with private schools, homeschooling isn't for everyone. It's plenty of work for parents, not all of whom feel they can adequately teach their children, especially at the high school level.

The good news is this doesn't have to be a once-and-for-all decision. It's sometimes a good idea to try all three. For example, home-school until age seven, private school through ninth grade, then public school until graduation, or some other arrangement of these three. Keep tinkering with your options until you find what's right for your child and family. Evaluate it each year and don't be afraid to entertain a different school option than that of your neighbor.

Choose Wisely

Whenever possible, take time to consider matters carefully before making decisions. When choosing a school, it is important to walk the campus and observe the students. What is the atmosphere? Do you like how the students are relating to each other and to adults? Interview the principal. What is the school's philosophy of education, and how is it being carried out? Are there special programs offered that interest you? You may want to observe in a classroom to help you make your decision. You are looking for an environment in which your child will thrive.

Respect Authority

Teachers appreciate students and parents who are courteous and follow the rules. Both you and your child will get the most out of every school experience if you remember to treat others as you want to be treated. Most educators want to help children and please parents. Make suggestions with a helpful attitude rather than a critical spirit. Kindness is not something we teach our children apart from example. Parents need to do their part in teaching respect to teachers.

Prepare Your Child for the Road, Not the Road for Your Child

Disappointments happen. Don't try to adjust or manipulate every situation so that your child will be successful. Instead, view each situation as a challenge to be met. Learning to overcome challenges is an important life skill. Some situations will really stretch your child, but usually that is when much growth takes places. If you constantly try to step in and change what seems difficult, your child may miss out on the opportunity to overcome and achieve in ways you never expected.

Change May Be Necessary

While it is important not to bail out of every difficult situation, sometimes change is necessary. The change may be as small as where your child sits in the class or as large as changing teachers or even schools. Sometimes no amount of effort will solve a problem. No matter how many positive reasons you have for staying, if your child cannot thrive, it is time for a change. Some changes are necessary for academic reasons. Some are necessary for social reasons.

Character Counts

Life is about more than school, and school is about more than academics. Treat the citizenship side of the report card as being very important. You should put more effort into teaching your child good character than you put into completing homework or special projects. It is far better to have a child with excellent character and less-than-perfect grades than it is to have a child who is academically superior and morally bankrupt. In all my years of education, I cannot think of a greater truth to pass on to preschool parents than what is found in Chapter Two of this book, *Factors of Learning*, particularly the relationship between moral excellence and academic success. There is a connection between the two, and poor is the child whose parents never make this connection.

Summary

As parents we have many reasons for wanting our children to get a good education. Our hopes and dreams for our children's futures seem to rest on their success in gaining a quality education. The preschool years provide a time to lay a firm foundation for education. The potential for success increases for the child who is developmentally ready for the school environment. His entire experience will be enhanced if his parents keep a clear, realistic, and proper perspective during these wonderful and adventurous years.

Chapter Eight

Laws of Correction for Preschoolers

Two four-year-old cousins were striking the dwarf plum tree with sturdy sticks. Laughing and chanting a nursery rhyme, the pair used their enchanted scepters to knock from the branches the newly formed plums. Too late, Grandma discovered and stopped their fairy-tale game. Previously, spring rains had wiped out all but a couple dozen plums. Now, nearly half of those lay on the ground.

Maybe you don't have plum trees, but chances are you have a child whose curiosity or mischievousness will lead him to commit an unwelcome deed. Let's face it—life is full of temptations. When your child discovers a hose in the yard, he will squirt water regardless of what is in his path. When your child sees pretty flowers, she will pick them regardless of whose yard they are in. If the library has "quiet rules," your child will scream. When it is time to sit, your child will move. There's no doubt that young lives require training. This is the reason we discipline our children. They must learn to live safely, wisely, and in a manner respectful of those around them. Part of this guidance comes from encouraging right behavior, and part comes from correcting wrong behavior. But what should correction for a preschooler look like?

In *On Becoming Toddlerwise*, we introduced the developmental concepts of *capacity* and *desire*. By way of review, we stated that childhood correction must align itself with age-readiness. For example, as demonstrated in Chapter Three, *The Voice Within*, we learned that the higher conscience of a child three years of age begins to develop and is ready to receive moral explanations. Your child is now intellectually ready to understand the "otherness" meaning of moral instructions such as, "Do not hit," "Do not steal," and "Do not lie." Therefore, parents have a much greater proactive role in virtue training. They begin to add moral explanation to their instruction in the process of building the child's moral warehouse.

In light of the absence of moral readiness, parents working with children prior to three years of age predominately work on outward behavior. That is, they help their child become familiar with right actions even though he is months away from understanding the moral implications of his own behavior. What are the developmental implications of these factors? It means that a child under two years of age is acting out of his nature and not from a moral sense of right and wrong. He clearly demonstrates a capacity for wrong, but does not have the knowledge of why it is wrong. While taking a toy from another child in the nursery is a "moral violation" and is a "moral action" that must be corrected, it is only a moral crime for the parent, not for the child. This is because parents are morally responsible because their toddler is not. For the one-year-old plus, it is simply the operation of his nature. He looks, he sees, he wants, he takes. He does not sit back and contemplate the rightness or wrongness of an action because such behavior for a one-year-old is valueless.

At three years of age everything changes. His behavior becomes value-driven. Now present is the capacity to understand right and wrong. This means that parents must now pay as much attention to issues of the heart that drive his behavior as they do the behavior itself. And that is why helping parents understand the basic laws of correction is as important in the developmental process as getting children ready for school. We will expand these concepts further in the next book in this series, *On Becoming Childwise*, but for our preschool audience here is an introduction.

We start our presentation by defining the word *correction*. In its simplest form, it means to bring back from error, or to "align an unacceptable deviation back to the standard." While parental encouragement *keeps* children on track and moving forward, correction is used to get them *back* on track. The correction side of discipline is guided by certain fixed principles. These are the fundamentals of correction, the filter through which all decisions regarding correction must pass. If you and your spouse are operating off these same principles, you will usually be able to come to the same disciplining conclusions without needing to take a time-out huddle or make an emergency cell phone call each time your child crosses the line. This is good news. Not only is the phone bill slashed in half, but your child gets consistent consequences no matter which parent is doing the correcting.

Regardless of your discipline situation, you can learn to administer correction fairly and effectively when you consistently apply to your thinking the Four Laws of Correction described on the following pages.

Law One: *Distinguish between Childishness and Defiance*

You are completely humiliated. Little Jenny delights in poking her head under the bathroom stall to see who's inside. Last time no one was there so you didn't fuss. This time, someone was. Suddenly it's a major violation and you wish you had stopped this game long before now. What is the line between innocent play and malicious behavior? When does curiosity cross the line to snooping? At what point does a misdemeanor become a felony? When do inappropriate actions become malicious disobedience?

If parenting were all about drawing lines, we would quickly run out of chalk. Fortunately, a thick black line has already been drawn for us in permanent ink. It marks the border between two totally separate realms of behavior. On one side is the *Land of Childish Mistakes*. On the other is the *Land of Defiant Misdeeds*. While the two lands have similar names, the difference between them is profound. The first speaks of nonrebellious acts; the second speaks of acts committed with malicious intent. Both require correction, but of different kinds.

There is a distinction between the child who accidentally hurts his brother while playing and the child who does so with the intention of inflicting pain. There is a difference between the child who accidentally damages property and the one who intentionally vandalizes. And there is a difference between bumping into a dwarf plum tree by accident and striking it with sticks to make the fruit fall to the ground.

The Ezzos have another fruit tree, this one a semi-dwarf grapefruit tree. It bears fruit once a year. In terms of size and color, the grapefruit look mature in November. However, they do not fully ripen until February and March. One Thanksgiving weekend, a group of three- and four-year-old children were playing in the back-yard. One child saw all the yellow grapefruit and thought he would help Mr. Ezzo by picking them. After all, last week he had helped his uncle harvest grapefruit (which came from a year-round producing tree), so he knew all about it—or so he thought. All the children joined in and picked a half-bushel of unripe grapefruit before their activities were discovered.

These children did not possess the correct information about the ripening process of grapefruits growing on a dwarf tree. Please note that it was lack of knowledge, not malicious intent in the hearts of the children, that drove their behavior. In fact, their intent was noble—to help Mr. Ezzo pick grapefruit. Their actions were simply *childish*. What they did was wrong, but they didn't think it was wrong. That afternoon, they received a lecture from their parents about touching what appeared to be ripe-looking fruit on trees without asking permission.

Let's look at the words *childishness* and *defiance*. We use the term *childishness* to refer to *innocent immaturity*. This includes those non-malicious, nonrebellious, accidental mistakes our children make —such as spilling a glass of water, accidentally bumping another person, or picking fruit from a neighbor's tree as in the case above. Childishness is when a child does something without knowing it was wrong. This action might be irritating to Mom and Dad, but wrong action doesn't become misbehavior until the child understands what it is that he did wrong. *Defiance*, on the other hand, implies bad motives. The child knew the act was wrong, but he did it anyway.

Childishness is usually a head problem—a lack of knowledge. Defiance is usually a heart problem—the child does not *want* to do the right thing. Eight-year-old Seth sneaked into the house looking for a good hiding place. Going from corner to corner with childhood glee, his foot caught a wire and a porcelain lamp crashed to the floor. Promptly, all the children were gathered together and told that the inside of the house was off-limits for hide-and-seek. With nods of understanding, they all went back outside. Twenty minutes later, Seth's six-year-old sister, Nicole, came sneaking into the house looking for a place to hide.

Now, Nicole did exactly what her brother did. Seth had entered the house playing hide-and-seek, and so had she. But there's a huge difference. Seth did it in childish innocence. Nicole did it knowing that she had just been told not to, defying her parents' instruction. *Motive* is what separates childishness from defiance. When instructions about something have been given and received, there is little room for "innocent mistakes" regarding that behavior. If the wrong thing is intentionally done, it's disobedience, outright defiance—pure and simple.

Parents should correct both childishness and defiance. But the form of correction will differ. When assessing a behavior in need of correction, parents should ask themselves, "Was my child's action the result of an accident, a misunderstanding, a lack of knowledge, or purposeful defiance or intent to cause harm?" How that question is answered will determine what happens next.

Law Two: *All Correction Must Promote Learning*
"Lindsey, don't splash your baby sister in the face," Mom says, only to see Lindsey wander across the wading pool to her next victim. *Splash. Splash.* Mom is shocked and the shouting ensues. If only Mom had explained the real issue behind Lindsey's first playful flick of water.

Correction requires explanation. Without the *why* (explanation) of wrong there is no correction, just a random redirection of behavior. Whether a child's actions are innocent mistakes or malicious disobedience, explanatory teaching will always be necessary. The parent's job is to give verbal explanation that moves the child from what he did this time to what he should do next time. Whatever the wrong behavior, use it to impart knowledge. If you complete your talk and learning didn't take place, correction didn't happen.

Don't be fooled. The reason five young children never picked unripened grapefruit again was not because they were severely punished (they weren't), but because they were made to understand why their actions were wrong. Knowledge that they formerly did not have became the basis of their future self-restraint. Often, imparting knowledge is the only correction that needs to take place.

Children learn by gaining knowledge, but not all knowledge comes through textbooks or living room lectures. Sometimes we teach our kids what not to do by walking them through behaviors. In the Ezzos' vegetable garden there is a series of brick walkways that children like to playfully weave through. Sometimes, however, little three-year-old feet mindlessly leave the path. Usually young children have no knowledge of plants underfoot. This child would not understand a lecture on the recovery rate of crushed cucumber stems. Education in this case is facilitated by hands-on learning—taking the child for a walk on the bricks, pointing out where he can step and where he cannot. Make the education you give age-appropriate. Just be sure to give it.

Children learn in a variety of ways. Sometimes the painful consequences associated with their actions become their tutors. Let's say your child ignores your instructions to not exit the swing in midair.

The resulting burn on his right thigh is a natural consequence. It teaches him the *why* behind your prohibition.

Consider the behavioral explanation you give today to be a deposit on tomorrow's behavior. Your goal is to transfer the motivation for right behavior from the external (you) to the internal (your child). That cannot happen without explaining to your child the *why* of behavior.

Law Three: *Make Any Punishment Fit the Crime*

It's natural for parents to react spontaneously to negative behavior. You see defiance, and boom, you jump on it. But before you jump in the next time, first stop and think for a moment. You must act for the child's good. Recklessly reacting in the heat of the moment isn't the best plan, nor does it get long-lasting results.

Where should parents begin when considering correction for their children's intentional disobedience? Disobedient behavior needs correction, but parents should not correct all disobedience the same way or with the same strength of consequence. Parents should modify their correction based on the following five factors.

- *The age of the child.* Am I training a preschooler who is just learning to put his world together or a fourth-grader approaching the middle years of childhood?

- *The frequency of the offense.* Is this the first time this offense has been committed in six months or the sixth time in six minutes? Correction should be handled with reference to frequency. If the first offense was handled at correction level one (whatever that may be in your home), the second, third, and sixteenth occurrences should be treated at progressively higher correction levels.

- *The context of the moment.* Context is not an excuse for disobedience, but it should be taken into consideration when determining consequences. Look back to the original incident to determine context. Did your child disobey as part of the group, or was he the leader of the pack?

- *The overall characterization of behavior.* Is this the only behavior in need of correction, or is it part of a larger pattern in need of attention? Is this the kind of thing your child often does, or was it some strange aberration? Is there some deeper problem that's causing this behavior? Perhaps you would be wasting effort treating a symptom of a bigger problem.

- *The need for balance.* When considering consequences, parents should also consider that overly harsh punishment exasperates a child, while excessive leniency fails to put a correct value on the offense. You know your child. Decide what level of punitive effect is appropriate for the offense, and take action that is calculated to achieve that effect.

Law Four: *An Offense against a Person or Property Requires an Apology*
A child's moral sensibility is intimately connected to his or her willingness to accept responsibility for wrongful actions. This awareness cannot be silent introspection. Teach your children to admit they are wrong when they are wrong. Walk them through it. Something as simple as "Sissy, I knocked your crayons on the floor" is a healthy

start and the first step in mending wounds.

Relationships work best when there is no unresolved conflict simmering within them. That is why this fourth law is so much a part of healthy families. Have you ever been offended by a friend, coworker, or family member when the person knew he had done wrong but refused to admit it? At best, he's just unusually nice to you for a while. That's his way of apologizing without having to admit his wrongdoing. But it's unsatisfactory.

You may not be able to change your coworkers, friends, parents, or siblings, but you can certainly train your children in this area. Think how these relationships bother you. Don't let it happen in your family between siblings or between your child and you. Humility is the basis for healthy family relationships. Seeking forgiveness for an offense and humbly admitting error in an effort to be restored with the offended party is a prerequisite for a loving and enduring relationship. This is serious heart business. People, regardless of age, who are in the habit of asking for forgiveness take ownership of their wrong actions. They show that they believe the relationship is worth the possible embarrassment often associated with admitting wrong.

In practice, what does an apology look like? What are the components? First, understand the distinction between saying "I'm sorry" and saying "Will you forgive me?" Both are appropriate, but both would not always be used in the same situations. "I'm sorry" is associated with unintentional mistakes, with childishness. Apologizing expresses regret over an action that caused hurt but was void of malice or hurtful intent. Seeking forgiveness on the other hand is appropriate when the person has willfully committed a hurtful act. There was intention to defy, injure, or destroy. This is a heart problem.

When four-year-old Kenneth unintentionally stepped in Mrs.

Brown's flower bed and uprooted a couple of new plants, his mom had him apologize by saying, "Mrs. Brown, I'm sorry for stepping on your flowers." That was an appropriate response since his actions were childish and devoid of purposeful wrongdoing. Kenneth's "I'm sorry" does not signal guilt, but rather his acknowledgment of the innocent wrong.

Let's change the scenario slightly and add a second dimension—instruction. We'll say Kenneth had received instructions from Mrs. Brown not to play near the flower bed. He even received an additional warning from his mother. But Kenneth chose to ignore both, leading to the trampling of the flowers.

In this case, his actions just leaped from childishness to defiance. His actions can no longer be blamed on innocent immaturity. In the first instance, he did not know any better. This time around, he disregarded Mrs. Brown's instructions and continued on a careless path. Simply put, he disobeyed.

Now a simple "I'm sorry" is not enough. Kenneth is compelled to a deeper commitment, that of seeking forgiveness. "Mrs. Brown, will you forgive me for playing in the flower bed even though you told me not to?" A matter of semantics? Not at all. The difference is great. To say "I'm sorry" is to acknowledge a mistake or acknowledge you got caught. To ask for forgiveness is to acknowledge a wrong motive of the heart. This is a humble acceptance of guilt. Mea culpa ("it was my fault") is a deterrent of the same negative behavior as much as any punitive correction.

Not convinced? Try it out in your marriage. The next time you and your spouse get to that place in a dispute where you are ready to make amends, seek out your spouse and instead of just saying "I'm sorry," try, "Honey, will you forgive me for losing control of my tongue?" or, "Will you forgive me for being so stubborn?" Difficult? You bet. Try it a couple of times and you will realize its healing power. You will find yourself guarding your tongue and actions more fervently. And that is exactly what happens with morally sensitive children.

Why is this forgiveness thing so powerful? Simply, it gets to the heart of the matter. When you say "I'm sorry," you are in control of that moment. You control the depth and sincerity of your sorrow. But when you seek forgiveness, the one you are humbling yourself before is in control. You're asking something of that person that you cannot get without his or her consent—*forgiveness*. It is this humbling effect that so wonderfully curbs a child's (and a parent's) appetite for going back and doing or saying the same wrong thing again.

To train this into your child, guide her to the phrase "Mom, I'm sorry" when she makes a mistake. When there is an act of defiance, teach her to ask forgiveness. "Sissy, will you forgive me?" In both cases, have her add on a *confession* of the specific infraction. "Sissy, will you forgive me for taking your toy?" Confession, as they say, is good for the soul.

This training will help cure your child of the "It was only an accident" sob story, which goes something like this. Mom says, "Honey, you need to say you're sorry to Mr. Franklin for knocking down all of the boxes." "But Mom!" Adam says, "I didn't mean to do it. It was just an accident. I shouldn't have to say I'm sorry."

Adam's thinking is the result of Mom's teaching that the phrase "I'm sorry" is good enough, rather than going the distance by adding "Will you forgive me?" When parents limit the options, they unintentionally force a child into unnecessary self-incrimination. If "I'm sorry" is linked to both innocent mistakes and purposeful wrong, then a child struggles with accepting responsibility for his honest mistakes.

In the scene above, Adam could not say "I'm sorry" because he would be admitting guilt to something he did not intentionally do. That is why separating childishness from defiance necessitates the two forms of apology. It keeps "I'm sorry" where it belongs, in the category of mistakes. A child is more willing to accept responsibility for his childish mistakes if he knows that saying "I'm sorry" will not falsely incriminate him. "I'm sorry" means one thing—that an individual (adult or child) is sorry for something he did. Seeking forgiveness, while more difficult, means quite another—that an individual is sorry that his actions or words hurt another person. The difference is huge.

Tools of Correction

When working on the engine of the car, or crafting furniture made of wood, every Dad knows that without the right tools the end result is often unsatisfactory. There are three tools of correction that are available to parents. They are:

- *Natural Consequences*—These consequences are not given by Mom or Dad, but are the result of the natural cause and effect of a situation. Mom hears the piercing screams of her four-year-old daughter, Abby. As she runs to the adjoining room, Mom sees the family cat, Tiger, sitting on her haunches glaring at Abby, who is pointing to the claw marks on the side of her face. Mom knows that Abby has suffered the *natural consequence* of teasing the cat. After the wound is cleaned and Abby's tears are dried, Mom gently takes Abby's small face into her hands and says, "Abby, I have told you many times you must not tease

Tiger. Now you know why. I am sad that you were hurt, but I hope that this will remind you the next time you want to tease Tiger that she might get mad and scratch you again."

- *Logical Consequences*—These consequences are determined and given by Mom and Dad. They must "logically" relate to the offense or they are not effective. Mom walks by the living room and sees toys scattered everywhere while her four-year-old son, Luke, stares zombie-like at the television. Mom sighs and says to Luke, "How many times have I told you to pick up your toys before you turn the television on?" Luke's response is, "I forgot."

Remember what we said earlier: Next time before you jump in, stop and think things through. Let's review what you have learned in this chapter.

- *Is this childishness or defiance? What is the frequency of the offense?* Whenever Mom starts a sentence with, "How many times…" it is defiance. Luke knows what he is supposed to do.

- *What is the age of child?* Luke, at four years of age, is capable of remembering to pick up his toys before he moves on to a new activity.

- *What is the child's overall characterization?* Luke "forgets" to do most everything he is asked to do. Is "forgetting" a legitimate excuse? Think about this—if you told Luke on Monday that you would take him to the neighborhood pizza palace on

Saturday and you do not mention it to him again, do you think Luke will on his own "remember" this promise come Saturday morning? You bet he will. Rule of thumb: Children will remember what is important to them and conveniently forget what is not.

This assessment points to the fact that Mom's reminding, nagging, begging, and threatening has gotten nowhere with Luke. He needs logical consequences to help him "remember" in the future. When thinking of what a good logical consequence would be, ask yourself what is it that your child has misused. In this case, Luke misused the privilege of watching television, as he hadn't picked up his toys first. So Luke losing the freedom to watch television for the rest of the day might be the best medicine for his memory.

- *Isolation*—We put a twist on the popular theory of time-out. When Mom gives her child a time-out for naughty behavior, Mom gives a time limit, usually one minute per year of the child's age. Frankly, it is not our experience that sitting in a chair for four minutes is sufficient motivation for a four-year-old child to learn to "obey Mommy." Next time, put your four-year-old in a chair in a place where he cannot be in the flow of household traffic. Let him know that when you can tell that he has calmed down and has his "happy attitude" back, you will come to him. When you go to him, this gives you the opportunity to put into practice what you have learned in this chapter. Ask your child if he is ready to apologize for his behavior. If he is not, then he needs to sit longer.

- Additional information on appropriate ways to correct a child can be found in the book preceding this one in this series, *On Becoming Toddlerwise*, and in the book following this one, *On Becoming Childwise*.

Summary

Correction is not about getting even with your child, but about training his heart. Your goal is to make the right path clear and, when necessary, to put the child back on it. To help cement these concepts in your mind and make them as much a part of your natural responses as possible, we invite you to work through the following scenarios. The purpose of this exercise is to help you become familiar with each of the Four Laws of Correction and the thought pattern necessary to bring fair and productive correction into your child's world. (You may wish to write on a separate sheet of paper.)

Scenario One

You come upon the scene described at the beginning of this chapter: Two four-year-olds are heaving at a dwarf plum tree with good-sized branches. The fruit is falling on the ground, where the children's feet grind them into a fine mush.

- Based on the First Law of Correction, in which category of wrong behavior did the children's behavior fall?
- Based on the Second Law of Correction, what type of education will prevent this behavior in the future?
- Does the Third Law of Correction apply to this situation?

- Based on the Fourth Law of Correction, what action is necessary to help bring closure to the children's wrong action?

Scenario Two

Now the hide-and-seek scenario: You catch six-year-old Nicole sneaking through the house playing hide-and-seek. You've already told all the children, including Nicole, not to play in the house. But her big brother, Seth, had just done the same thing only minutes before. His behavior resulted in a broken lamp. Nicole hasn't broken anything yet.

- Based on the First Law of Correction, into which category of wrong behavior did Nicole's behavior fall? What about Seth's behavior?
- Based on the Second Law of Correction, what could you do to help educate both children?
- Based on the Third Law of Correction, what should their parents consider?
- Based on the Fourth Law of Correction, what action is necessary to help bring closure to Nicole's wrong action?

How We Handled These Situations

Because these were actual events, we thought it would be useful to record what the authority figures actually did in these scenarios.

Scenario One

In the plum tree incident, we were dealing with childishness. Kara and R. J., the four-year-olds in question, had no malicious intent to do harm, nor an understanding of the cause and effect of their actions. They did not equate their present action as having significant meaning to others. However, though Kara and R. J.'s actions were void of malice, they nevertheless did bring injury to another's property.

Grandma took both children (with their sticks) and showed them what they did wrong. She then took them to another tree, the grapefruit tree, and showed them how wrong it would be to strike this tree. She extended the lesson to the rosebushes. "You don't strike the plums, the grapefruit, or the roses," she said.

Additionally, the children lost the privilege of playing with their magical sticks and had to pick up all the plums. Finally, the children were directed to Grandpa, where they both apologized "For knocking down your plums, Grandpa." Since that time, neither we nor their parents have ever faced that behavior again.

Scenario Two

Although it was a costly accident, Seth's behavior was just that— an accident. His actions were considered childish, not defiant. Nonetheless, he was required to help clean up the mess. He was also at an age that made it appropriate for him to help pay something toward a new lamp. This was part of the learning experience. Although he did not mean harm, Seth had to learn to accept responsibility for his unintentional actions, as well as the intentional ones.

Nicole's behavior, on the other hand, was not childish, but defiant. She simply ignored the instructions previously given. For her complete disregard of the instructions, she was punished. The *logical consequence* applied taught her the importance of submitting to parental leadership. She lost the privilege of playing the game. Seth was guided to apologize to his parents, sharing how sorry he was for his carelessness. Nicole was guided to seek forgiveness for her rebellious heart actions. Both children were returned to the right path.

Chapter Nine

Odds and Ends and Helpful Tools

Sometimes you just need something extra. Even Mary Poppins with all her charm relied upon a spoonful of sugar to "help the medicine go down." And while we cannot promise you toys that march themselves to their box, we do have a few nifty tools of our own. Bearing in mind that every child is unique, often requiring an added measure of effort in specific areas, we offer the following ideas to boost positive, controlled training in the life of your child. These ideas work to make life for you, the parent, a bit less turbulent. Your child a joy to be around.

Quieting the Wiggles

Do you have one? You know, a mover and a shaker, a high energy, perpetual motion, chase-his-own-tail kid. How many times have you tried to slow your little missile down with words such as these: "Calm down," "Settle down," "Sit still," "Stop moving," "Stop kicking," "Put your hands down," or "Sit on your hands"? Has it ever worked for longer than a millisecond?

Have you ever thought about what "settle down" or "slow down" looks like to a three-year-old child? These are abstract concepts, metaphors. A three-year-old doesn't have a clue what you mean. Louise called her friend Jessie in a moment of desperation. "Jessie, I'm getting a little apprehensive about our breakfast meeting with the Ezzos this Saturday. My two little ones do not do well sitting for long periods of time. Help!" "Louise," Jessie said, "there is a nifty little thing that helps children gain self-control in moments when you most want it and they most need it. Are you ready?" "Yes!" came Louise's response. Jessie continued, "When you begin to see those early signs that your kids are going to lose it physically or verbally, instruct them to fold their hands and work on getting some self-control. That is all you need to do."

Louise began the training immediately. She and her family did meet the Ezzos that Saturday for breakfast. Toward the end of the meal, a little wandering leg propped itself up on sister's chair. That would normally be enough of a catalyst to energize the two-and-a-half-year-old and four-year-old into all-out playtime right there in the restaurant—but Mom had another plan. Instead of the classic begs, bribes, and threats, she simply said, "Girls, we're not quite ready to go yet. I want you to fold your hands and get some self-control."

Would you believe that in less than a minute those two little girls sat still, with their hands folded in their laps, subduing their impulsive behavior? And this without a war of words with Mom! Mom then pulled out some crayons and let them color on the paper napkins. Teaching your child that self-control begins with the folding of her hands is a wonderfully concrete way for her to understand calmness. Her eyes focus on those peaceful hands lying still in her lap, and soon physical and verbal self-control is achieved.

On Ounce of Prevention

Parents should always try to help a child gain self-control *before* he crosses the bridge of trouble, not afterward. The hand-folding exercise does exactly that. It is a wonderful tool that can be used at grocery checkout counters, school functions, sporting events, dentist's offices, or during that longer-than-usual sermon.

When a young child folds his hands to get self-control, it handles all the excessive body energy that makes self-control so difficult. After all, if you want your child to settle down, his energy has to go somewhere. Now, instead of it going into squabbling, cartwheeling, or whispering, it can go into the hands.

Another amazing thing about hand-folding is how quickly it brings about self-control. Usually only thirty to ninety seconds needs to elapse before Mom can say, "Okay, kids, you can let go of your hands." Your child only needs to fold her hands long enough to gain self-control in that moment. Once that is accomplished, Mom can redirect the child's energy to productive activities (like coloring on paper napkins).

It is important to teach this technique to your child when things are calm. If you're already in the conflict, your children are not going to be especially attentive pupils. You may have your child practice this at the table while you finish up last-minute mealtime preparations. Make it a fun game in the beginning. Demonstrate how to achieve self-control during a peaceful time so that when things begin to get out-of-hand, you've got the cure in place.

This simple technique will become second nature to your child and will work wonders in creating the peace your family deserves.

Slow, Slower, and Slowest—Teaching the "Three Candy Speed"

Your little guy's dentist appointment is in just a few minutes. You completely forgot about it last month, so you want to be on time. All you've got to do is have your son pick up his markers and put away his paper. You instruct him to do so. He gives you a nice "Yes Mommy" and begins to clean up.

But for some reason you feel like you've entered the Twilight Zone. Right before your eyes, your son, who normally has all the energy in the world, suddenly goes limp on you. He moves slower than the 1950's movie *The Blob*. "Sammy, you have to pick up your crayons right now." One marker is picked up. *Pause*. Another marker. *Yawn*. "Come on, Sammy. Now! I mean it. We have to get going." One more marker. *Pause*. Another marker. *Scratch*. "Sammy, move faster! Sammy, we're going to be late because of you. Come on, Sammy, move faster!" For Mom, this whole episode has transformed into a slow-motion dream. Each of the boy's limbs seem attached to an invisible stretchy web, pulling against him as he reaches for the marker's purple cap.

What's happening here? Clearly, he sees your rush to get out of the house. You prompt him, reminding him to hurry so you don't steal the dentist's time by being late. You find yourself rambling on with insignificant, energy-draining adult reasoning until you are ready to scream. Instead, you clean the coffeepot, stick some glasses in the dishwasher, nervously glancing over your shoulder at the clock, then at your son to check his progress. You know he can move faster. But how do you get him to pick up the pace without sounding like a slave master?

The problem is that your preschooler doesn't know what "fast" looks like. It's an abstract concept. *Three Candy Speed* is a way to show him what accelerated movement is. Surely if your child's favorite candy waited at the end of his task, you'd see lightning-fast movement on his part. You might be thinking that we are encouraging you to bribe your child. Not at all. Keep reading!

Try this sometime when you're not rushed. Begin with a slight mess that your child needs to pick up. Put three small pieces of candy on the counter, and call your child over. Tell him that you are going to set the timer and that he should begin cleaning up when you do so. Inform him that if the toys are picked up and neatly put away, these three pieces of candy will be his reward. At this point, his energy is on full alert and he takes his mark. Go! The child moves faster than you've ever seen, thus beating the timer. This is his *Three Candy Speed*. You just established in concrete form a benchmark of time that becomes a future reference point for you both.

While Sammy is consuming the candy (and before the sugar rush kicks in), sit him down and explain to him that the speed he just moved at is called *Three Candy Speed*. You need to tell him that he will not be getting candy every time you ask him to do something. In fact, this is the only time he will get candy for moving fast. Tell him you just wanted him to feel himself going fast so that later, when you need him to move quickly, you can just tell him to go at *Three Candy Speed*, and he'll know what that feels like. The next time you need to get moving lickety-split, all you have to do is tell him to pick up his toys at *Three Candy Speed*.

Positive Speech

We approached this subject in *On Becoming Toddlerwise* and will do so again in *On Becoming Childwise*. The reason we repeat it here is that it is developmentally important that parents know how to speak positively to their children. Preschoolers are spirited little beings, always on the go. They give us plenty of reason to keep our guard up, and as a result we spend as much time restraining wrong behavior as we do encouraging right behavior. While words of restraint are necessary throughout the training process, we must also attempt to communicate with positive words, especially during the preschool phase of our child's life, where the foundation of language is being expanded. Being positive in your speech will take self-discipline on the part of Mom and Dad, but it will pay great dividends.

When communicating with your children, attempt to speak as often as possible in the positive not the negative. If there is something you don't want your child to do, then communicate your desire in the positive. As often as possible use the negative of the virtue, not the negative of the vice. Did you get all that?

Surely if any concept needs explaining this one does. Most "wrong" behavior is broken into the vice or virtue category. The vice category is negative; the virtue is positive. If a child does something wrong, parents tend to describe the negative side of the vice. For example, a parent will comment to her four-year-old son, "Hitting your sister was foolish." Foolish represents the negative of the vice. But when you use the negative of the virtue (positive), you would say, "Hitting your sister was unkind." Unkind is the negative side of the virtue. Instead of saying, "You're lying" (the negative side of the vice), consider, "You're not telling Mommy the truth." Instead of saying, "You're acting selfish," consider, "You're not thinking of others." Using the negative side of the virtue is far better than using the negative side of the vice when describing a child's lack of courteous behavior.

You can use positive speech in other ways. Here are a few more examples. Instead of saying:

- "Don't spill your cereal on your way to the table," *say*, "See how carefully you can carry your cereal to the table."
- "Don't get out of bed," *say*, "Obey Mommy and stay in bed."
- "Don't talk so much," *say*, "You need to learn to become a better listener."
- "Don't leave a mess for everyone else to clean up," *say*, "Be responsible and clean up after yourself."

With preschoolers there will always be plenty of justifiable "don'ts." "Don't touch the knives." "Don't play with the stereo." "Don't hit the dog." "Don't go near the road." Such spoken prohibitions are appropriate and necessary with young children. But as a child matures, he needs positive direction from you. As you get into the habit of using positive speech, when you do need to be negative, such as, "Don't run into the street!" your child will respond more quickly. Consider the transfer from negative to positive speech a good habit to get into.

Pre-Activity Instruction: Ask and Tell

Before you go to the store, library, church, or music class, it is helpful to give your child a pre-activity instruction. Before you leave the house, crouch down to your child's eye level to get his attention and then go over the "Store Rules." Tell him what you expect his behavior to be while you are out. "Store Rules" might include:

- Hold Mommy's hand at all times when walking to and from the car.
- Stay by Mommy's side when shopping.
- No touching.
- No asking for Mommy to buy a toy or treat.
- Obey Mommy.

Once the rules are understood and become a habit of your child's thinking process, you can reverse the process. Instead of telling your preschooler what is expected of him, ask him to tell you what the "Store Rules" are. This is a great way to refresh and remind your child of your expectation while you are out. In addition, it helps him internalize these expectations as well.

There are a number of settings where you can utilize the "*tell and ask*" approach. It might be a person rather than a place. Greeting the librarian is a good example. You are working on verbal courtesy with your preschooler. On the way to the library you might say, "Now Joshua, when we see Mrs. Anderson (the librarian) she will say hello to you. You should look up into her eyes and say hello back to her." When you believe that your child is capable, approach encouragement using the imperative form of direction: "Joshua, tell me how you will greet Mrs. Anderson when we see her today." Please note that you are not asking Joshua a question: "Joshua, can you tell me how to greet Mrs. Anderson?" Rather, you are directing him to give the answer he knows to be correct. This is a productive way to reinforce habits of courtesy.

A variety of courtesies can be taught by using the *"tell and ask"* approach. Moral scenarios will include saying "thank you" when receiving a compliment or seeking permission before playing in Mrs. Jones' backyard, or with her puppy, or when desiring to be excused from the table, or whatever other courtesy is socially and morally appropriate. The more consistently Mom and Dad employ this technique, the more ingrained the habits of courtesy will become in your child's life.

No Whining

"I want a snack. Mommyyyy, I want a snack." Mom silently wonders if her daughter will ever stop whining. The most effective way we have found to deal with whining is to have your child ask for permission (in a cheerful tone) for the things he wants. The reason your child whines is because at some point you give in to him, just to stop the whining. Think about it. If you are going to give in, wouldn't you rather it be to a child who has cheerfully asked you if he can have a snack, rather than to one who has demanded it from you in an angry or whiny tone?

Teaching your child to ask for permission for what he wants or wants to do will lesson the need for correction at a later time. Your child will quickly learn that having Mom's permission to play outside is better than Mom finding him outside when he was supposed to be picking up the toys on his bedroom floor. "Mommy, may I please...?" Now that's sweet music to every parent's ear!

Tools of Encouragement

Parents all over the world have found the following three activities to be a great way to motivate children to do chores, care for others, and be responsible.

Cheerful Chore Cards

Let's face it, getting kids to do their chores can be tiresome. Mom is constantly prodding and endlessly checks for progress; the children are stalling, whining, and bickering. It almost makes a parent want to just give up and give in.

Family chores play a significant role in building loyalty, unity, and responsibility into your child. Therefore, parents must find a way to work through the agony of getting a child to do his chores for future rewards. Connie Hadidian, author of *Creative Family Times*,[12] offers a creative approach to accomplishing family chores for preschool-age children.

You'll need colored three-by-five-inch index cards, an index card box, three-by-five-inch dividers, and a black marker. Divide your chore card box into four sections. Pick one color to use for each child's personal tasks (i.e., blue for Matthew's personal tasks, red for Rachel's). Personal chores include making the bed, brushing teeth, picking up the child's room, etc. Choose another color to represent chores that preschoolers are capable of doing (we will give a list of suitable chores for preschoolers later in this chapter). Paste or draw a picture on all the cards to represent the task or chore you want your

---

[12]See Allen and Connie Hadidian, *Creative Family Times* (Moody Press, 1989).

child to be responsible for. Finally, pick a color of cards to be used as special "See Mom for a treat" cards.

Here is how it works. Each morning, Matthew's chore cards are placed out for him on the kitchen table or the counter. This will consist of his personal task cards and his chore cards. Mom sets the kitchen timer for an appropriate amount of time. Matthew works through his cards, flipping each facedown when the task is completed until all chores are done. They must all be done before the timer goes off.

The last card in Matthew's stack reads, "See Mom if you think you are done." This card is helpful for two reasons. First, it lets you know if the chores are done before the timer goes off, and second, you can check to see if the job is done to your satisfaction. Every once in a while, Mom throws in the special card, "See Mom for a treat." When your child discovers this, after his squeals of delight die down, express your appreciation for how well he is doing. The special treat might be going out for an ice cream cone, a dollar bill, or some other small treat.

Here are some advantages to this method:

- It takes only a few minutes each morning to gather the children's chore cards for the day, or you can put them out the night before.
- It teaches children responsibility and self-discipline.
- The system is flexible. You can add or delete chores as needed and as your child grows older.

Here are a few more samples of chores age-appropriate to preschoolers:

- Dress themselves
- Make bed
- Wipe up their own minor spills
- Help set and clear table (do not expect perfection)
- Put dirty clothes in hamper
- Pick up socks and shoes
- Empty small wastebaskets
- Dust baseboards and bottom of kitchen chairs

While none of the above will be accomplished exactly the way you would like, these activities are getting the child into the habit of tidiness. Keep it simple, stay with it, and please remember the following helpful guidelines.

- Don't expect him to do the task alone the first time. Work alongside him until he understands what to do and how to do it himself.
- Do less and less for your child as he becomes more and more responsible.
- Praise your children for great attitudes and jobs well done!

Finally, regarding motivation, remember that simply getting outward performance is not the goal of your parenting. The goal is to help create a servant's heart in your children. Chores are one way to teach the virtue of *otherness* (putting the needs of others before yourself). Your children need to feel that they are important contributing members of your family. Having them do chores is one way to accomplish this, and yes, it can start as early as age three.

Charting Positive Action

By using the principles in Chapter Eight, *Laws of Correction for Preschoolers*, we believe you will begin to see progress in the correction arena. However, sometimes we all need something a little extra. The *Positive Action Chart* is a nifty tool that can move a child from the not-doing-wrong stage into the spontaneously-doing-right stage.

This calls for the creation of a colorful chart. Make a special trip to the craft store with your little one to purchase the needed material. Let your child help create the chart, as this will further enhance his ownership of it. Select poster board and markers and a variety of fun-filled stickers. Before creating the chart, consider specific traits you would like to see developed in the heart of your child. Love, joy, peace, patience, kindness, goodness, faithfulness, gentleness, and self-control are good starting points. These form a portrait of a tender heart that looks to the needs of others before his own.

On the left-hand column of your chart, list the attributes we mentioned above. Write the days of the week across the top. Now post this chart in a prominent place in your home. The kitchen is a good place, or your child's bedroom—if you don't mind him dragging every visitor into his room to check out the cool poster the two of you created.

Here's how it works. Each time your child demonstrates one of the positive attributes on the chart, you point it out. You explain exactly what happened and how it relates to the desirable trait. He gets to put a sticker on the chart. When you start actively looking for, say, kindness, you may find it where you least expect it. This can be surprising to moms who have been focused on restraining the negative behavior of their preschoolers. Watch how your child's face lights up as you begin to notice the good, inspiring actions he does every day. This will encourage him to keep up the good work!

For areas of development where your preschooler needs extra help, offer bigger stickers when that trait is demonstrated. For every ten stickers that are accumulated on the chart, a reward is given. This may be a trip to the ice cream parlor, or purchasing a new book. When fifty stickers have been accumulated, create a wonderful memory for your child to savor, such as a trip to the zoo. The encouragement he receives from seeing his own virtues mount up is worth more to him than any scoop of mint chip or visit with a chimpanzee. However it is nice to be rewarded for the good things he does! Being recognized for a job well done is a major shot in the arm in his journey toward the kind of character any parent could be proud of.

Marbles for a Cause

There are days when Mom feels like a referee, sorting out battles between siblings. Much of this strife is caused by tattling. "Mommy! Justin hit me!" is a frequent refrain heard in homes where more than one child resides. We have another helpful tool parents can use to promote harmony in the home.

Get a large plastic jar and a bag of marbles. Whenever anyone catches another family member doing something good, he gets to put a marble in the jar on behalf of that person. When the jar is full, the family chooses something fun to do together. When another family member puts a marble in the jar because your preschooler did something good, this alone is enough immediate recognition to inspire similar behavior in the future. Do not think of this as a type of bribe. The difference between a bribe and a reward is this: A bribe is offered up-front. Beth gets a piece of candy *before* she picks up her toys. That's a bribe. A reward is given *after* the desired behavior occurs. Beth gets a piece of candy *after* she picks up her toys *because* she did so without being reminded. That's a reward.

To avoid dependency on rewards, some ground rules must be established. First, no one gets to put a marble in the jar because *he* did something good. Someone else has to notice another's goodness. Second, there may be no complaining if a child's "good deed" goes unnoticed. Sometimes life will be unfair. But that is when you teach your children that we all should be willing to do good things, not for the praise of another man but simply because it is the right thing to do.

Before you start, you must actually consider what the desirable traits look like in order to not overlook too many. For example, following through on a task is faithfulness. Not crying when a treasured candy is dropped and crushed in a carnival stampede is surely self-control. Playing nicely together for a prolonged period of time brings much-treasured peace. And sharing a new birthday present with another anxious onlooker demonstrates love. Take a few minutes during dinner for family members to share the good things other family members have done. When Mom and Dad agree that the thing mentioned is worthy of a marble, then the child gets to put it in the jar.

Manners at Mealtime

Back in the colonial days of horse and buggies and Southern plantations with moss dangling trees, visitors to country estates sometimes traveled days to their destination. As a result, these guests would often stay on the plantation for weeks at a time, enjoying the company and hospitality of their host. As it happens today, sometimes guests overstay their welcome. In the plantation days, the master or mistress of the home would never be so uncivil as to ask their guest to leave. However, there was a way to communicate the message.

At one of the meals, the guests would be served a cold shoulder of mutton or ham, which usually had a higher fat content and thus was less desirable. When the guests received this "cold shoulder," they knew their welcome had come to an end, and a few days later they would be on their way. While some social customs surrounding meals have changed over the years, gracious mealtime behavior is never out of fashion.

Children acquire good manners in two ways: through education and instruction, and by parental example. The latter, of course, is as important as the first. If Dad asks Mom to "Please pass the potatoes" and then replies to Mom with "Thank you," such courtesies are easily accepted by a preschooler as integral parts of his speech and patterns of behavior.

The context of mealtime is one of the best for teaching courtesies that have lasting social value. They are "other-regarding" rather than "self-regarding" and hence become a useful tutor in preparing a child for *otherness* virtues that are necessary to get along with others. In short, good manners become an integral part of a child's character, and thus a well-mannered child is a gift returned to society. Good manners will always accompany good morals. Children with good manners shine brightly wherever they go. While sitting with your children in a restaurant, you just might hear the voice of a stranger comment, "What well-mannered children you have. They're so polite." Such compliments are the result of correct training in social graces, particularly in mealtime etiquette, and they are well worth the effort.

Etiquette refers to one's behavior in the presence of others and should manifest itself in a demonstration of courtesy, politeness, and respect. Your goal is to train your child in such a way that he practices these courtesies both at home and away. Listed below are some basic recommendations of politeness and respect as they relate to mealtime behavior. Here are some general courtesies to work on with your kids.

Positive mealtime manners include:

- Complimenting the cook
- Chewing quietly, keeping your mouth closed
- Saying "Please" and "Thank you"
- Not leaning on the table
- Not reaching across the table
- Not stuffing your mouth
- Not talking with your mouth full

Recommendations for Various Mealtime Settings

There are five mealtime settings families will experience. They include:

- Dinner at home with no guests
- Dinner at home with guests
- Buffet-style dinner with guests
- Dinner away from home as guests
- Dinner at a restaurant

Keep in mind, most of these settings require practice at home for a period of time before your child tries his manners on others. Look for conflict-free opportunities and comfortable avenues for introducing these different environments. Invite close friends over specifically for this purpose. Ask your mother if she might have you over for lunch, especially if you have an outing on the horizon in which you wish your children to shine. Practice! And remember, your example does make a difference. Don't get so focused on your child's behavior that *you* forget to praise your Mom's cooking, the table setting, placemats, or centerpiece. Anything that seems appealing will resonate in your child's mind and provide fuel for future compliments he will make.

The following etiquette suggestions can assist you in training your children in gracious mealtime behavior. Mealtimes provide opportunities to teach and learn about the social graces of politeness, preference, and respect. The following are our recommendations.

Dinner at Home with No Guests

- No one begins to eat until all are seated. This is a very tangible way to show appreciation to the cook and server.
- Children should eat what they are served.
- Children may not play with their food.
- General requests such as "I want more potatoes" should be changed to "Mom, may I have some more potatoes, please?"
- Whatever a little finger touches he must eat. If your child touches a piece of chicken while exploring the plate, he gets the first piece he touched. In this way he shows respect to those he shares the meal with and also learns the social importance

of a serving fork and spoon.

- No one starts to eat dessert until the server sits down and joins the family. Everyone eats together. This is similar to the first point above and communicates both appreciation and respect for the server.

- No one leaves the table until everyone has completed their meal. Children especially need to ask their parents to be excused from the table.

Dinner at Home with Guests

In addition to the above, the following two recommendations will help emphasize the importance of showing hospitality and respect for those outside the family who are joining you for a meal in your home.

- Teach your children to prefer your guests by offering food to them first. This is a form of hospitality and a sign of welcoming your friends to your table.

- Again, children should not leave the table unless first excused by parents. They should then acknowledge the adult guests with, "Excuse me, Mr. and Mrs. Smith." This is a picture of courteousness.

Buffet-Style Dinner with Guests

Here are few suggestions for entertaining in a buffet style when at home:

- Whenever practical and possible, invite the oldest guests to go through the line first. This is a wonderful gesture of respect for age.

- After the adult guests serve themselves, the children are assisted by the hostess or parents.
- The host and/or hostess should be available at the buffet table for serving and directing. Their presence and supervision will help keep things orderly.

Dinner Away from Home as Guests

There are two additional recommendations that will help your children recognize and respond appropriately to the hosts when in someone else's home for a meal.

- Children should not to begin serving their plates or eating until the host or hostess directs them to do so. This shows respect for the host/hostess.
- Children should not leave the table or wander around unless they ask the host or hostess to be excused (after asking Mom or Dad for permission first).

Dinner at a Restaurant

Taking your children to eat in public settings is not a problem when sufficient training has taken place at home. Added to the recommendations above, this single guideline fits the restaurant scene.

- Keep dining out simple and limit it to good fast-food restaurants until your child is able to demonstrate social courtesies and politeness in more formalized settings. After all, you are sharing the restaurant with others who are in hopes of enjoying a meal.

• Do not let your children be disruptive or rude. And please remember this—while your child's actions may be cute to you, other diners may not agree with you.

Understanding Childhood Fears

How old were you when you first saw the ghoulish monkeys dispatched by the Wicked Witch of The West to pick up Dorothy and her dog, Toto? Do you remember the scene of winged monkeys spreading the gentle Scarecrow "here, there, and everywhere"? These scenes from the movie *The Wizard of Oz*, when observed by this writer, were some of the most frightening scenes that a twelve-inch black-and-white screen could project to the pounding heart of an eight-year-old boy.

Fear! It is part of the overall human experience and not simply a childhood phenomenon. Some childhood fears might appear irrational, even silly, to parents because they do not arise from any real external danger, but they are very real to the child and should be respected as such. Although the cause of fears may not always be discovered, we know there are general categories of fear that children experience. Knowing the origin of fears may not always eliminate them, but it may lead parents to better management and reduction of fearful stimuli. Consider these sources:

• *Natural Fears*—In spite of the fact that fears vary from child to child, there is evidence that certain fears are characteristically found at specific ages. These are referred to as "typical fears."

Many fears are learned from direct association of experiences with fearful stimuli. The most frequently displayed fears for preschoolers come from animals such as dogs, snakes, and rats. These are followed by the fear of strange people, being left alone, and dark or high places.

- *Fear of the Unfamiliar*—Among the primary fears of young children is the fear of the strange and unfamiliar (strange from the point of view that something stands apart from the child's previous experience). It could be a person, event, situation, or activity. This type of fear takes place because young children do not have cognitive tools to adequately measure the legitimacy of their fear and thus lack the ability to understand the cause and effect associated with fearful situations. For example, a child with an ice-cream cone may not understand that it was the food that attracted the neighbor's puppy and not a wolflike desire to devour the child. Yet the fear, although misplaced, is still very real in the mind of the child.

- *Developing Imagination*—We have already discussed the developmental benefits of a child's imagination in Chapter One, *Children Need to Play*. Imagination can also create fearful expectations, especially when the imagination develops faster than the child's reasoning abilities. Imaginary fears include ghosts, skeletons, bogeymen, or any combination of the above.

- *False Beliefs*—Some fear is the result of bad experiences, such as the fear of the dentist or the hospital or a visit to the doctor's office. The frightening experience becomes an expected reality and thus apprehensiveness occurs. Your child will even react with fear to a new situation that, in and of itself, normally would not arouse fear. Other fears are passed on to children by the false beliefs of their parents, siblings, and friends.

- *Parental Anxiety*—Parents sometimes unwittingly arouse fears in their children and introduce attitudes of apprehension by their own overprotective anxiety. Constant warnings of restraint such as "Be careful, you're going to fall down," "Don't pet the dog or he will bite," "Don't climb in the tree or you will fall and break your leg," or "Don't go by the road you might get hit by a car" might keep a child in an atmosphere of fear and continuous dread.

Note the operative word above is *constant*. Of course there will be times in which you might say all of the above. This is not the same as constant warnings of danger that place a child in a perpetual state of anxiety about his own welfare.

Helping Children Manage and Overcome Fear

Some fears need to be managed, while other fears can be overcome with time and education. Here are some facts and suggestions to consider while working with your child's fears.

- *Fear itself is not a cure for fear*—Forcing a fearful preschooler to "face his fears" is not the best way to help him overcome them, nor is ridiculing a child for being afraid or commanding him to ignore his fears. This approach goes against the very thing the child needs—that being the full confidence that his burden of fear is being shared with Mom and Dad or big brother or sister. Ridiculing and name-calling are antagonistic forces to companionship and trusting relationships.

• *Education*—Methods that promote self-confidence are the best ways to help children overcome their fears, and this can be done in part through education. Children are less likely to be fearful if they have some understanding of the object of fear. When the child learns that the puppy's actions are playful not threatening, and that the snake is behind the glass and cannot get out, or that thunder has an explanation, he will better be able to manage potential fear with the assurance brought by such knowledge. Educating a child about his natural fears is one of the best ways to reduce fear that parents can use with their child.

• *Getting acquainted*—Giving your preschooler opportunity to get acquainted with the fearful object or situation is another form of education. This may take time since the child's confidence in the knowledge of what is safe must grow stronger than the fearful experience of the past. Gradually introducing your child to the object of dread through role-playing, actual encounter with the object, or parental example helps alleviate his fears. When your child sees that Mom is not afraid to play with the puppy, he will join in the fun and in time overcome his fear. In contrast, if Mom overreacts to the excited puppy by hopping on a chair, the child will not be far behind her.

• *Removing fearful stimuli*—Remove all inappropriate fearful stimuli from your child's life. *The Wizard of Oz* is not a movie for preschool-age child to watch. Even the movie *Dumbo* can create apprehension. Poor little Dumbo, separated from his Mom and forced to work the circus scene as an oddity, is way beyond the context of your preschooler's sense of security. Take note of what your child is watching on television, including cartoons. Given the state of the world, even the nightly news can be fear-provoking to children (and adults).

• *Substitution, not just suppression*—Universal in application, this particular suggestion should not be limited to the single category of fear, but applied to any circumstance that employs moral and virtuous opposites. For example, the Ezzos were once approached by a father asking how to deal with his son's obsessive jealousy. That question leads to a broader one—how do you deal not only with jealousy, but all attitudes of the heart and emotions, including fear? Children of all ages are better served by substitution than by suppression. The father mentioned above was frustrated by his efforts to suppress his son's jealousy. No matter how hard he tried to keep the lid on it, jealousy continued to leak out.

The problem here and for many parents is not simply the presence of a vice or a weakness, but the absence of a virtue and strength. Suppression of wrong behavior is often achieved by encouraging the opposite virtue. (Remember what was said earlier in this chapter about *positive words*?) If you want to suppress jealousy, give equal time to elevating the opposite virtue, which in this case is contentment. If you have a child struggling with envy, teach charity. For anger, teach self-control. For revenge, teach forgiveness. Substitution will make all the difference in the world.

This same principle applies to childhood fears. Often the problem is not the presence of fear but rather the absence of courage. Parents, by the language they use, tend to focus primarily on the fear (the negative) and not on courage (the positive). Instead of saying, "Don't be afraid," parents should consider saying instead, "Be brave" or "Be courageous." This type of encouragement is not meant to satisfy a moment of fear, but to establish a pattern of belief for a lifetime.

• *Prevention*—Most of the suggestions above that can help overcome fears can also be employed to prevent many fears. Giving a child a heads-up about the neighbor's dog or how loud the fireworks will sound makes good sense. When dealing with young children, some form of pre-activity warning is better than the shock of discovery.

Considering the fact that children's fears are not in essence greatly different from those of adults, parents should demonstrate great patience toward a fearful child. Do not put a premium on insisting that a child not be afraid, but assure him that you will walk with him through fearful situations. After all, the last thing you want to create is a condition in which your child fears telling you about his fears.

Community—How important Is It?

Fittingly, we conclude this book with a word on the anthropological need all human beings have for *community*. The term *community* can mean many things to many people. We use it to refer to a group of families sharing common interests, values, and a significant commitment to an ideal for the mutual benefit of the individual and the collective membership. In other words, to quote the Three Musketeers, "*All for one and one for all!*" Why is it important to have a community? Because a community does something that nothing else can—it establishes a sense of "we-ness" in the group that encourages members to work toward a common good. It provides a sense of belonging and association. As we've seen in our large cities, where virtually everyone is unknown to everyone else, the absence of we-ness causes accountability to disappear—and with it common morality. That will always be to your children's detriment. Where there is no common standard to strive for, there will be limited expectations of your children.

Since members of your community are going to teach your preschooler (directly or indirectly), it is vital that you surround yourself with people who are like-minded and share your standards of virtuous training. In a moral community, you will find people who are striving to demonstrate respect and honor as part of their daily life and to instill in their children a moral awareness and consideration of others. These are the people who can provide a support group for you, Mom and Dad.

A like-minded moral community will insulate your child against unfriendly elements. Through association with like-minded peers, your children will see family standards reinforced by others who share the same values. The strength they draw from peers with similar moral values is the very thing that makes it possible for you as parents to let them participate in activities such as a community soccer league. You want to recruit a child of like-minded friends to enroll in the kinder-gym class with your child. When all other children are running around, it will be easier for your child to sit as the teacher has instructed if he has a buddy who will sit with him. The support of a moral community allows our families to be a blessing to others because we know that the moral strength we draw from our like-minded community allows us to present something very beautiful to the world.

Your children will find his or her friends in your community. You want those friends to be moral kids—kids whose Moms and Dads are working to instill values in their hearts just as you are with your child. A like-minded moral community is vital. As your child works through the preschool years, his interests will broaden and his attachment to friends will become more meaningful. Over time he is becoming morally and relationally emancipated and self-reliant. That is why the moral community to which you and your child belong will either be a friend or foe to your family values.

Children do better when the community they grow up in reinforces the values the parents are trying to instill. The greater the disparity between the values of your family and your community (from which both you and your child will draw peers), the greater the source of conflict within the home. The opposite is also true—shared values between community and home result in positive peer pressure on your child. Think of it. Other children holding your child to the standard is much more preferable than peers destroying almost overnight the virtuous training you worked so hard to instill.

The Power of Age-Related Wisdom and Community

Sociologists say that America will have a shortfall of qualified laborers in twenty years. As baby boomers begin to retire, there will not be enough new workers around to fill the void. Solution? Go back and hire some of those aged baby boomers and utilize that good old-fashioned wisdom that only life experience can bring.

In ancient Israel, town elders sat at the gate deciding matters of importance. When men and women living in those times needed counsel on the sale of property, help with a business investment, or wisdom on how to deal with a troublesome child, they knew where to go. They went to the city gate, the place of the elders. Today, we still need counsel in all these areas. Sadly, though, we have lost respect for the "aged ones" who could guide us so wisely. Think about it. Who are the elders at your gate?

Having a moral community is important. But we're going to take this idea one step further and tell you that not only do you need a community that includes peers; you also need a community that includes elders. Is this an old-fashioned idea? You bet it is. And one in need of social resurgence.

Think for a moment about the people who are in your family's community. Within that mix, who are the parents who have gone before you? Where do you get your wisdom: from the media, television talk shows, from public opinion—or from those who have gone before you successfully? Who are the elders in your community? Not only is it good for you, Mom and Dad, to have this resource; it is also comforting for your child to know that Mom and Dad have someone older and wiser they go to for advice. As you seek the wisdom of elders, you are setting a silent example. Your child sees that you understand your need wisdom from an elder who knows what you are going through. As a result, your child will be more inclined to come to you than to peers when the need for guidance arises.

It may not be immediately apparent who your elders are. You may have to look around. Where do you begin? Start by considering your grandparents and your parents. How can you involve them in your lives? Your parents or grandparents may not be living in your area, however it is likely that someone's grandparents live in your community. Invite them to your home for a meal. Tell them what you're doing. Embrace them and their wisdom. Ask for their advice.

Summary

Whether you are teaching self-control, revving up your child's engine, or training into the heart those positive traits you desire for the life of your child, be creative. Be loving and fun, bearing in mind the principles for training presented in this book. There is a place for correction, stern admonishment, and clearly defined boundaries. Yet in weeding out the wrongs, don't neglect to plant beautiful seeds, watering them with encouragement and praise. Then your child's heart truly will blossom. Implement the above helpful tools with wisdom and patience. Adapt them to suit your situation. Start with one and add on as desired. Each is backed by validated success and proven track records from parents like you, looking for an added boost in the right direction.

Appendix A

Toys and Things

Toys! How can a parent know how to pick and choose through the vast array of toys and games available for children? We can help! We are providing a review of many age-appropriate toys and games for your preschooler. While the list is filled with good ideas and worthy advice, please do not underestimate the power of your child's imagination. Although educational toys can help stimulate the mind, no toy can match the power of a child's creativity. Before you run out and spend a lot of money, consider the treasures already laying around the house.

Do not throw out the box your washer or refrigerator came in. Where you see a piece of cardboard, your child sees an adventure waiting to be experienced. The box becomes your daughter's "Little House on the Prairie" sitting in your living room. It floats the high seas as a pirate ship, or moves through the neighborhood as a fire engine. From secret hideouts in Robin Hood's forest to Dad's downtown office, that box is anything your child's imagination chooses to make it.

Imagination is a tool of the mind. Hours of imaginative play come about with the everyday items we so quickly discard. A 2 x 4 plank of wood cut up into blocks, patches of colored fabric, an empty tea kettle, or those throw-away plastic plant pots can all find a purpose in your child's imagination. We believe if parents use a little imagination with the common objects just laying around their home, a child will create uncommon adventures that toys purchased in stores could never produce. Look around your garage, attic, and basement. Fun items are just waiting to be discovered.

Guidelines for Choosing a Toy with Lasting Value
Jenice Hoffman, Contributor

- *The toy calls upon a child's imagination and encourages imaginative play*. There are many toys available today based on children's movies and cartoon serials. While some imagination will be employed, your children for the most part will mimic what they saw in the movie, instead of creating with their imagination. These toys promote pre-programmed play. Children watch the show and the reenact the show through the toys. While this in and of itself is not bad, neither is it sufficient. Ask yourself, "What is this show teaching my child?"

- *The toy is durable*. Toys that are easily cleaned, repaired, and re-used year after year give you the best value for your money. Ask yourself, "Will the toy last longer than the box it comes in?" If you suspect it won't, don't buy it.

- *The toy is challenging and stimulating, without going beyond the child's skill or maturity level*. Most toys provide a recommended age-range as part of the packaging. Parents should pay attention to the guidelines. The manufacturers have put in months of testing with children to come to these guidelines. Do remember the recommended ages given are guidelines. If your child is struggling during playtime, consider that the toy may be above or below his skill level.

- *The toy is child-powered.* If a non-battery-powered toy is avail-able next to one with batteries, opt for the one that your child must manipulate and power himself. A child-powered toy requires a child to engage himself physically and mentally, which stimulates creativity with the toy. For the most part battery-powered toys require adult supervision, which limits when the child can play with it.

- *The toy has long-lasting "play value".* A toy should hold a child's interest and interaction for years, not minutes. Many toys on the market are "play specific", meaning they have one use, one action, one role. Choose toys that can be used in multiple ways. Blocks are a good example of this.

- *The toy is a safe toy.* Always look for small parts, edges, projec-tiles, and other potential dangers should the toy break. Cloth toys should be treated for flame-resistance. Painted toys should be painted with non-toxic paints. In most cases, A toy should not require constant supervision to ensure safety or correct use by the child. Don't buy a toy without looking at it. Many peo-ple buy toys based on the box or packaging. Open the box and evaluate the contents for yourself.

- *The toy results in happy dreams and a healthy soul.* Do not buy toys that promote occult behaviors, (such as crystal balls or Ouija boards). We would recommend that you stay away from toys rooted in fear, such as monsters, ghouls, ghosts, goblins, or gross-fantasy creatures.

- *The toy can be shared to promote group interaction.* Many toys are geared for children to play with by themselves. Choose toys that invite children to play together, communicate with one another, and share experiences, ideas, decision-making, and problem-solving skills in a team format.

- *Young children are not qualified to choose toys.* Children are often influenced by advertising, packaging, cartoons, and peer pressure. Children's ideas of what they want change each and every day. Toys should never be purchased as a symbol of social status. We are not saying that a child should never get to pick out a toy at the store, but that adults should use discretion. Ask your child if he is willing to spend his allowance on the coveted toy. If not, then don't be quick to spend your money. Also, it can be beneficial to have a child wait a few days to see if he still wants a particular toy.

Toys for Boys or Girls

Below are suggestions of toys we find educational, entertaining, and fun for children. This list is by no means exhaustive. It is meant to give parents ideas on where to start when determining which toy would be appropriate for your child. We encourage you to consider purchasing toys at garage and yard sales, where they can be found for a considerably less amount of money that at a store. Be sure you thoroughly clean used toys before giving them to your child. Also, mention of a particular brand name below does not necessarily exclude other brands. The ones mentioned are familiar and easy to find.

Balls

A ball is a toy that your child will enjoy from infancy to adulthood. It is perhaps the most universal of all toys. Preschoolers can get a lot of enjoyment from inflatable beach balls.

Blocks

Manufactured blocks have been around as a toy for nearly three hundred years. Undoubtedly they go back to the days of ancient Rome, Greece, and Egypt. With that fact alone, we have to assume that blocks are a great way for children to creatively play. Blocks come in all kinds of shapes, materials and sizes.

- *Wooden Blocks*—These are normally recommended for children over 2 years-of-age. Younger children enjoy blocks but should only have access to products without a painted surface.

- *Waffle Blocks* (Little Tikes)—They are ideal for indoor and outdoor play. These are simple interlocking blocks for building in three dimensions.

- *Duplo Blocks* (Lego)—These are some of the most engrossing and enduring toys a young child can own. They come in a large assortment of colors, are easy to clean, and allow a child to build whatever his or her imagination will think of. They are perfect in size for little hands to play with.

Games

As children get older games are a wonderful way to teach socialization skills such as taking turns, friendly competition, luck, and simple strategy skills.

- *Candyland (2 years and up)*
- *Hi Ho Cherrio (2 years and up)*
- *Chutes and Ladders (4 and up)*
- *Memory*
- *Boggle Junior*
- *Pick-Up sticks (4 years and up)*
- *Children's Monopoly (5 years and up)*
- *Dominoes (6 years and up)*
- *Scrabble Junior (6 years and up)*

Playsets

Little people playsets (Fisher Price, Playmobile, Little Tikes) have become the mainstay in toy boxes of children 2 to 6 years-of-age. The Garage, Farm, Airplane, and School Bus are just a few that are available.

Traditional Favorites

We can't help but reflect on some of the toys that we enjoyed as children, and those toys are still some of the most creative and popular today.

- *Play-Doh*—This timeless favorite is great because it can be used on days when the weather makes it impossible to be outdoors. With young children, be sure to take the time to sit down and show your children what to do with the Play-Doh.

- *Bubbles*—Bubbles are for outdoor play. Young children are fascinated by them!

- *Slinky, YoYo's, Hula Hoop, and Jump Rope*—Additional favorites that have stood the test of time.

Toys that can be Ridden

From swings to rocking horses to bikes, children love toys that can be ridden! Little Tikes makes wonderful toys for riding. A rocking horse is a wonderful addition to any child's room.

Musical Instruments

Musical toys are geared towards enhancing children's creativity and encouraging them to explore the world of music and their own talents and giftedness. Please know that there is a vast difference between musical instruments that are manufactured as toys and those that are not. Children should not be allowed to play with musical instruments that are not toys without first having formal instruction or lessons. It is great fun to put on some music, hand your preschooler a tambourine and watch him march!

- *Piano*—Toy pianos and keyboards are popular with children.

- *Rhythm Instruments*—Musical instruments that are made especially for children such as tambourine, hand bells, castanets, harmonicas, kazoos and recorders can be found at any music retail store.

ON BECOMING PRESCHOOLWISE

- *Audio-Tape Cassette Player*—Around the age of 3-4 years a child can learn to be responsible with a audio-tape cassette player. There are several on the market geared just for children. Parents need to use their discernment when it comes to CD players, as CDs scratch easily and are not durable.

Puzzles

Children will spend hours playing with puzzles. The following are types of puzzles available.

- *Knobbed Puzzles*—These are puzzles with knobs on the puzzle pieces to help children grasp at the puzzle. Children can start to play with these around 18 months-of-age.

- *Floor Puzzles*—The entire family will enjoy working with these.

- *Board Puzzles*—Some have peek-a-boo boards so that another image appears as the puzzle pieces are removed.

- *Wooden Puzzles*—Another wonderful way to start your children off with puzzles. These are very durable for little hands.

Toys for Boys

- *Carpenter Sets*—Boys love to pretend to be like Daddy. Tools and carpenter sets that are manufactured as toys can be among a little boy's favorite toy.

- *Tool Benches*—Little Tikes and Fisher Price have two of the best tool benches available.

- *Real Tools*—As your boy get a little older, you can pick up a small tool set from Real Tools that looks just like Dad's or Grandpa's.

- *Tonka Trucks*—Tonka now makes cars and trucks for children of all ages. A dump truck is normally the best truck to start out with, and then you can move to more complicated trucks.

- *Brio Trains*—These are a great investment. Around 2 years-of-age, little boys can enjoy playing with these types of wooden train sets. Other well-known manufacturers include Thomas the Train, TC Timber, and Sesame Street.

- *Hot Wheels/Matchbox*—Hot Wheels and Matchbox cars a very durable. Both manufacturers make fun accessories as well.

- *Wooden Vehicle Model Kits*—Child craft has kits to start teaching your children about putting together models of vehicles. This activity should be supervised by an adult.

- *Brio Mech*—A form of Erector sets, made of wood instead of steel. Children from 3 years-of-age and up will enjoy these.

- *Tinker Toys*—A wonderful first building set for young children. For children 3 years-of-age and up.

- *Lincoln Logs*—A building toy that has stood the test of time. For children 4 years-of-age and up.

Toys for Girls

- *Dolls*—Little girls virtually always see dolls as their own babies, putting themselves in the 'Mommy' role. Dolls provide a valuable means of role-model training and an outlet for play related to behaviors children will carry into adulthood. Dolls come in all shapes, sizes, and colors.

- *Skill-Teaching Dolls*—There are a lot of dolls now on the market that teach your child how to button buttons, zip zippers, and fasten buckles.

- *Heirloom Dolls*—Many parents like to start a collection of dolls for their daughters. The American Girl and Madame Alexandria dolls all fall into this category. These dolls are not for young children.

- *Paper Dolls*—These type of dolls come in many varieties, including fabric and magnetic forms.

- *Doll Accessories*—A doll is not enough for little girls to play with. Your daughter will want a doll bed or cradle, stroller or buggy, and diaper bag.

- *Doll Houses*—A house full of miniature everything! Popular brand names are Fisher Price, Little Tikes, and Playmobile.

Full-size doll houses and kitchen sets are fun if you have a place to put it.

- *Dress-Up Clothes*—Girls love to dress-up. Scour garage sales and goodwill stores for evening dresses, costume jewelry, shoes, and hats.

Children and Books

Children and books go together in a special way. It is hard to imagine any pleasure greater than a young child curled up on Mom or Dad's lap walking through an imaginary adventure in the form of a story. Children don't stumble onto good books by themselves; they must be introduced to the wonder of words put together in such a way that they spin out pure joy and magic. It is great when parents can take the time to read through a book first and make sure that it is appropriate for your child.

A good book is a magical gateway into a wider world of wonder, beauty, delight, and adventure. Books are experiences that make us grow and add something to our inner stature. Quality books purchased now become an investment in future generations. Here are some tips to encourage your children to become good readers:

- *Keep Books Handy*—Create places around the house to keep books visible to your child. The bottom of a bookcase in the family room, plastic bins, and wicker baskets work well. Make a list of books you would like to have in your home. We keep a few out of reach to insure that they will be preserved through the years. Trips to the library are an adventure and can bring in a new supply each week. When a relative asks what to get a child for his Christmas or Birthday gift give them a list of books you would like to have.

- *Choose books with your child's interests in mind*—Embrace your child's interests by finding books on topics that fascinate him. Do remember that what is of interest to a preschooler will quickly change. Be flexible.

- *Read at bedtime*—We strongly encourage fathers to take an active role in their children's routine. For most Dads, bedtime is one of the best times to have a special time of reading with young children.

- *Read after mealtime*—Before the kitchen table is cleared off and the last aromas of a great meal dissipate, get into the habit of reading right after dinner. Keep the stories age-appropriate, interesting, and short. (10—15 minutes is plenty)

- *Talk about the story as you read*—To ensure your child is following along with you, ask him questions about the story. If the story is set in a city, talk about how the pictures of buildings in the book look like buildings in your town. Explain things as you read that you don't think your child understands.

When There are too Many Toys

Children tend to accumulate a lot of stuff! Trying to keep track of all their possessions, scattered here and there can be overwhelming to a preschooler and Mom. That is why we suggest limiting the amount of toys stashed away in your child's closet. It is just smart parenting. When you see that your child has lost interest in a toy, put it away for a while. Store it in a plastic bin somewhere out of view and reach of your preschooler. If he doesn't ask for it over the next few months, he probably has outgrown it. Save it for the next child or give it way to a friend, a charity, or put it in your neighbor's garage sale. This is also good way of getting rid of those annoying toys. There is no law that says you must keep the obnoxious burping frog just because Uncle Chuck thought your 4-year-old would love it.

There are different season during the year when toy collections for the less fortunate take place. Take advantage of this. If you are wondering if another toy could even possibly fit into your child's room, here is a timely way to involve your preschooler in the act of giving. Ask your child what toys he would be willing to give to an underprivileged child. Knowing that preschoolers love to give, this might serve as a tender teaching moment about the preciousness of others.

Tidying Up

A preschooler is certainly capable of picking up his toys. But he needs both teaching and encouragement. The following are some age-appropriate suggestions. First, when it is practical, set up some guide-lines for the play objects. Instructing your 3-year-old to "Pick up your toys" at the end of the day, when toys are scattered everywhere is ask-ing too much of him. No wonder he sits down with the exclamation of "I can't!" Therefore, limit how many of any item may be out at one time. Some of our preschool Moms permit only five crayons out of the box at one time when coloring, or one puzzle board on the floor, or four Hot Wheels on the track. As a child submits to the wisdom of such limitations gradually increase the number that you are comfortable with as long as he is able to clean up after playtime with out falling apart emotionally. Find the right balance for your home and child.

A second suggestion is to have designated places for all toys. There are some bedroom toys that only stay in the bedroom, basement toys that stay in the basement, and garage toys that stay outside. Plastic see through boxes are great places to store and sort toys of similar interest and purpose. Code you boxes with color tape. Blue boxes are for puzzles only, while the green box are for play station accessories, and the red taped box for trucks and cars. Color coding also facilitates the educational skill of "sorting" which a one of the skills your child will be tested on during developmental placement at age four.

Finally, a word to the weary Mom. There will be days when you are tired of parenting, feeling overwhelmed, too poop to care, and wondering if there may have been a baby switch at the hospital right after birth. It might just be time for you to turn off the television, shut down the computer, forget about the laundry, get a babysitter and go to the movies.

Don't forget—parents need to play too! Mental, physical and emotional fatigue does not make for a happy mother, or blissful parenting. Find time to relax and get away. Charge up your batteries with a weekly date night, once a quarter overnight away, or mini family vacation where the sights and sounds of life are different than the clamor at home.

Appendix B

The Land of Good Reason

Authors Note

Many times during the writing of this book, we found it appropriate to reference different portions of "The Land of Good Reason" as it appeared in *On Becoming Toddlerwise*. Because the contents of this chapter is not age specific, but covers broad general concepts associated with decision making and parenting, an editorial decision was made to bring the entire chapter forward as an appendix in this book. We trust it will be as helpful to you as it is to our *On Becoming Toddlerwise* readership.

Opinions on how to raise a toddler are easy to come by. Just type "toddler" into your Internet search engine, and you will find more than 900,000 options. Twenty top listings are highlighted for greater speed! This is great news if you are in a hurry, but which one do you read first? Whose advice will you believe? What options fit your family's identity? By the time you sort it all out, your toddler will be 22-years-old and pouting over a down payment on a house.

The ease with which parents can find a ready-made solution might be part of a bigger problem within our society. Whenever there is a surplus of easily accessible knowledge, there is a corresponding downside—the reduction of critical thinking skills, leading to atrophy of thought. The less skillfully you think, the more others will think for you. From the viewpoints of an educator and a medical practitioner, this chapter might well be the most important for many of our readers. It's not one *filled with* answers to your toddler questions, but it shows you how to *find* your answers. It's not a "*how-to*" chapter but a "*how-to-think*" with good reason chapter.

This chapter is all about problem solving. How do you decide what to do in the moment of toddler conflict or needs? What is the best prescription for your toddler's wandering hands or little feet: encouragement, correction, diversion, or isolation? What playgroup should he be in, or what freedoms should he have? How do you know where to draw the line? How do you know you're making the right decision for the long haul? What do you base your decisions on?

This chapter is not about *how* you parent, but *why* you do what you do, and what happens to your thinking when the all important *why* is removed.

Consider these very real toddler scenarios. What if it is your toddler who:

1. Runs toward the street, ignoring your calls to stop.
2. Gets out of bed before you awake in the morning.
3. Pats your newly washed sliding doors with his sticky hands.
4. Cries every time you drop him off at the nursery.
5. Is told to stay out of baby sister's room, but is found climbing the sides of her crib.
6. Is caught taking toys home from the neighbor's yard.
7. Tells you that he does not have to go potty and then messes his pants.

What would you do in each situation, and why would you do it?

The Land of Good Reason

Imagine a faraway land where you face situations with satisfactory solutions, free from self-doubt and second thoughts. This the "Land of Good Reason," where keenly interested parents find rest and encouragement and answers to their toddler questions. In this place where beautiful ideas dangle ripe and the Southern breeze wafts gently, dwell the *Rationals*. These are people who know how to find reasonable solutions to the unreasonable behaviors of the little people living in their homes. The Rationals understand that little people present unreasonable behaviors in need of sensible solutions. This neither alarms them, nor causes distress.

Does the Land of Good Reason seem impossibly unreal to you? It need not be that way. The use of rational deduction to make sound parenting decisions in moments of testing is a tool of reason, and "Good Reason" awaits every parent keenly interested in finding reasonable solutions. As you will read, found within a delightful melody known to all Rationals is the secret of reasoning well.

Over in the Land of Good Reason, the Rational mother tucked in her little wanderer for an afternoon nap. Then she settled back in her sea-green lounger, footrest popped up, to gaze upward and outward through her glass-topped abode. Her windows were open so the breeze drifted through as she hummed a melody she learned as a child.

"Believe in your beliefs," she softly sang. "Trust that your goals are true. Then you'll know why you try what you try. The truth behind effort serves you." Slowly, and rhythmically, the mother, nearly dozing, repeated the sweet refrain. Eventually, and with no particular haste, a most splendid parrot swooped this way and that over the glass-top home, catching the Rational's attention at last. Having alerted her of his presence, the lovely green creature circled down and around to the window ledge next to the lounger.

"Hello, beautiful parrot", she said in greeting.

"Beautiful parrot. Yes, beautiful parrot", he answered on cue.

"Tell me, my parrot, about my beliefs", said the Rational, still dreamy and soft-spoken.

"Beliefs. *Beliefs with goals* equal *why,* add *how* and you come to solve your problems," the parrot rattled.

"Thank-you," said the Rational mother, picturing the formula in her mind.

BELIEFS + goals = WHY + how = Solutions to (toddler) needs.

With this confidence, the Rational laid back and closed her eyes, content with this confirmation of beliefs connected to the problem at hand. "Believe in your beliefs. Trust that your goals are true," hummed the peaceful Rational, enjoying what remained of the day's restful period. "Then you'll know why you try what you try. The truth behind effort serves you."

Not far from the Rationals was the village of the poor *Howtos.* They had their methods, but knew little of *why.* Once, these lovely people shared a common ancestry with the Rationals. But suddenly struck by a devastating storm called *Need,* the Howtos became isolated from the Land of Good Reason. Many of their sages and elders were swept away in a flood of information, leaving the Howtos isolated from the ways of the Rationals.

Lost forever in the storm of Need, the wisdom of old became buried in the sludge of doubt and fear. The storm washed in new seeds of old habits. Soon a forest of habits grew so thick and dense that seldom did the Howtos see the light of day, and seldom did they dare venture beyond their clustered village. No beautiful parrots ventured over to this land, as the canopy of habits was uninviting and the light of day too weak. Instead of thinking for themselves they fell into the habit of letting the council think for them.

One day sitting on her front stoop, a weary Howto mother pondered deeply, "My grandmother used to sing the song of the Rationals. Within the lyrics is the formula that can free me from this forest of Habit. How did that song go?" She mused over the lyrics. "Dream of how to find a solution? Or was it, Believe in your habits? No it was, Dream about your habits. No, no, I must know this song. Ah, tonight I will summon the Council of the Wise."

Impatiently she waited for dusk to settle in over the ridge, and then she took out her wee little fife and beckoned for the council. They swooped in by the hundreds—owls of every size. Some had wide brown eyes encircled with thick white downy feathers. Others were small and brown, plain looking to the natural eye. Some gray ones sat high above the rest, looking down. Eagerly, she asked the multitude of owls to recall for her the parrot's old song. "Please, dear council, might you share with me the parrot's teaching on the little people?" Then respectfully she sat on her doorstep to listen intently, eager to hear the sweet song of old.

"Parrot?! What does she mean, summoning us to discuss some puffed up imitation of guacamole? This woman has nerve," flapped the first gray owl to swoop down before the frightened Howto. "Pipe down, old fool," flared up a larger brown owl, plump and cheerful. "Don't get those new feathers ruffled. These pitiful creatures count on our, ahem, expertise." Then turning to the Howto woman, he inquired with feigned sympathy, "What is it you want of the parrot's teaching my dear?"

"Well, I..., I..., I just know the sweet peace of the song my grandma would sing as she fiddled with daisies in her garden. I never met the parrot, really, and I don't mean to offend you. I just thought if I could only...," she rambled, her voice weakening and drifting off, lost in the growing grumbles of the council. "Well my dear, if you must know the truth, danger awaits those who think too much. Get everyone thinking, and what do you have? Shambles! That's it. One does this, and another tries that. Before long, they're all reasoning things out on their own. Then, who's listening to the council of experts? Who? Who?"

"Shame on you and your fragile ego," said a distinguished old gray owl. "I know the song of which you speak, my dear. It is the song of the Rationals."

"And how do you know these words?" laughed a smaller brown speckled owl with a trendy tie. "You venture this poor Howto mother to folly. It will do no good. Habits cannot be changed."

The Howto mother glanced up at the thorny trees and sought out the large creature. "Hush, all of you!" he demanded. The gray owl settled in with a bob and a sway, stretched his neck with a twist, and turned and spoke with dignified slowness. "I knew of the ways of the Rationals." He paused. "Their village is close. Before the flood of Need, I lived in their trees."

The forest clamored with hoots. "You have not spoken of this before," piped up a rather dull looking owl with darting green eyes. "And if their village is so close, why have we not seen these creatures?"

"No one asked before," returned the old gray owl. "Their village is just outside the Forest of Habit. No Rational would venture through the foreboding forest, for they know that to do so is to get lost in the way of Habit."

He turned again to the Howto mother. Slowly the song of the Rationals burst forth from the old owl as he swayed on the top branch. Clearly, this was the song of old. "Believe in your beliefs. Trust that your goals are true," he sang to the enraptured Howto. "Then you'll know why you try what you try. The truth behind effort serves you." At this, the forest fairly shook with nervous giggles and grins of fellow owls. Slowly, the Howto mother pondered and then turned, enthralled by her discovery. "The formula!" she called out. "It is there. Beliefs. Goals. *Why*, then *How*. Here in the land of Howto we only know of *how* but not *why*, and *why* comes from the union of our *beliefs* and *goals*."

From one Howto mother to another, the song was repeated again and again, and it caused the old habits to die off. The light of day grew brighter as the canopy of habit pushed back. Soon the beautiful parrots came reciting their wisdom to all who would listen.

"BELIEFS + goals = WHY + how = Solutions to (toddler) needs"

What can we learn from this distant land? While imaginary talking parrots and owls live in the land of enchantment, you and I live in the here and now. But the two villages very much represent parenting styles true to this day. Dwelling among us are the Howto parents, who know much about the way of parenting. They have formed comfortable habits. They have their methods and allow no substitutes. Their mantra is *just show me how*. How do I stop these sticky fingers from touching the clean windows? How do I stop this child from running toward the street? How do I keep this child in his own bed? Once they have the *how*, they never think of the *why*.

The *how/why* Dichotomy

The word *dichotomy* is often used to express a puzzling contradiction. The word actually has a specific technical origin in logic, astronomy, botany, and zoology. It has wrongly been taken over by writers whose only idea of its meaning is tied to fallacies, i.e. *false dichotomy*. The word comes from the Greek *dikhotomia*, a splitting into two, and in English it originally referred to a division into two strongly contrasted parts. This is how we are using it.

We begin with a question. What values or virtues do you deem important? We all work from a hierarchy of assumptions and beliefs. If you were to diagram a personal pyramid of values, what would be at the top of your list? What would be ranked second, third, and so on? What convictions do you hold? What goals do you have for your children, family, marriage, parenting, employment, friends, or matters of spiritual importance? Parenting is made most difficult if the answers to these questions remain nebulous, distant, or unimportant in your thinking.

Once you identify your beliefs and goals, you have the **W** in our equation—the *why* of our behavior. The next symbol of the equation is where the rubber meets the road in parenting. It is taking the *why* behind what we are doing, based on our beliefs and goals and translating it into *how* we accomplish our *why*. In other words, *why* is the value, and *how* represents the many options of application. *How* is what will get you to your goal. Most importantly, *how* has value only to the extent that it can satisfy *why*.

To understand the *how/why* portion of our formula, we introduce a common workplace example.[13] Suppose your supervisor sends you a memo asking for copies of the financial report. He needs the report for the directors, who are meeting right after lunch. You step into action. How will you satisfy the supervisor's request? You probably take the report to the copy machine. Or, if the line is too long, you might take the project to a local copy service downtown. You could even print the reports from your computer. The method used to duplicate the report, the *how*, serves the value of *why*. In this situation, you might ask yourself, "Why am I duplicating this report?" The answer is that there is a board meeting, and you were instructed to provide copies for all the directors.

When *how* Tries to Take Over *why*

One of the most unrecognized causes of frustration in the management of the home or the corporate office appears when *how* takes over *why*. We mistakingly and unintentionally assign value to *how* and then let it supercede the greater value of *why*. How easy is it to let this happen? Let's go back to the copy machine example.

The supervisor asked you for copies of the financial report. You go over to the photocopier and push *Start*. You process a few pages, and then the red indicator light begins to flash. What will you do? Of course, the first thing we all think of is to fix the copy machine.

---

[13]This wonderful concept was first shared by Joe Barlow, a friend of the Ezzos. He learned it from his father, Daniel Barlow and his mother Teresa Barlow, who both applied it to the workplace and the successful rearing of their fourteen children.

You open the paper trays, check for jams, remove the jam, and reset the machine. Again you hit *Start*, and again the red light flashes. Frustrated, you open more panels, clear the rollers, check the toner, shake the paper, and start over. Another jam occurs. You call a few friends over to help you. They suggest calling the copy repair service. Now your controlling passion is to fix the copier.

But if we were to stop in that moment and ask, "What was the original *why* that led me to the copy machine?" The answer would be, "To duplicate the report." Is there another way you can duplicate the report? Yes, you can go next door and use the neighbor's copy machine, or as suggested above, go to a copy center, or try printing the copies of the report from your computer.

Here is the point. Sometimes the *hows* of life stop us cold. Out of frustration we begin to examine why our method (*how*) does not work, and we miss moving forward in life because we are stuck on a broken *how*. The secondary *how* then begins to dominate our thinking and consumes our time and our emotional energy. We end up worried and more focused on fixing the *how* than returning to the original *why* to consider other means to satisfy it. In fact, we often become spellbound by fear that if our *how* does not get fixed, our goals will never be achieved.

What does *why* do for us? It keeps us focused on the hierarchy of our values. In our scenario, the greatest value now is not fixing the copy machine but getting the report duplicated and to the directors' meeting on time. The *how* is secondary and only serves the primary *why*.

In parenting the greatest values are not on *how* you accomplish your goals, but the *whys* that govern your goals. *Do not lose sight of the why of your parenting.*

At the risk of repetition, but in hopes of making this point very clear, consider this second personal illustration. Recently Anne Marie and Gary met with their neighbors and friends, Harold and his wife Nancy, at the boat launch on the river. They pulled the boat out of the water and securely cinched the bow to the trailer. The wives moved into the truck to find relief from the swarms of mosquitoes while Harold and Gary went to the back of the trailer to harness the stern. (Tying down the stern is done as an added measure of security when towing the boat.) With mosquitoes attacking their unprotected legs, arms, and heads, Harold, an old-time South Carolina gentleman, took one side and Gary took the other. In a few moments Harold was done, but Gary could not get his cinch hook to tighten. He took the strap off, he examined it, reversed it, and tried it again, all the while swatting at mosquitoes. He still had no luck. Taking the cinch in his hands, he examined it like a craftsman examines a fine piece of wood, reversed the strap configuration, refastened the trailer hooks, and pulled hard. The straps gave way. Harold just stood there looking at him. Gary gave it another try but to no avail.

Then Harold, in his Southern gentleman's way, asked, "What's the problem?"

"Cinch strap won't grab," Gary responded.

Harold's no-nonsense response rescued Gary from the *how* of his situation and met their need to get away from the festering mosquitoes. "Use the stern rope hanging over the side in front of you," he said to Gary.

The stern rope? Why didn't Gary think about that? It was dangling right in front of his nose. It even got in his way once. His frustration with a broken cinch strap prevented him from seeing the obvious. Gary was so consumed with the broken *how* (the cinch strap that had worked effectively before) that other alternatives to satisfy the original *why* (securing the stern) were not even considered.

How easy it is to get caught up in the *hows* of life and let them replace the more important *whys*. Harold's simple suggestion brought Gary back to the original *why* of his actions: to secure the boat.

This unfortunately is exactly what happens in parenting. We get so caught up with methods of parenting that we forget the *whys* of our parenting. We let the servant *how* become the master over *why*, and that locks us into a process of frustration leading to potential failure. The **H** changes the value of **W**, and we can never come to the best workable solution. Caught up in the forest of habits, we find a solution that might work in the moment, but there is doubt, second-guessing, and the lingering thought, *"did I handle this right?"*

Unfortunately, many a mom and dad stop right there—at "How to," which is primarily made up of *how*. These are the Howto parents. For the Howto mother, learned resolutions are everything. Night and day, day and night, she ponders the overwhelming dilemma, asking, "How? Show me how." Incredibly and most clearly, the Howto mom never stopped to consider *why* she was so bothered by the windows smudged with peanut butter. Was the obstructed view such a huge dilemma, or were there other, deeper issues and behaviors of greater concern?

In a recent conversation, a Howto mother commented to Gary Ezzo that she found herself frustrated when spanking her three-year-old, since it appeared to have no lasting effect on his behavior. She asked Gary what she might be doing wrong. The conversation went like this:

Mother: "Spanking doesn't seem to be working. What am I doing wrong?"

Gary: "Why are you spanking?"

Mother: "Because I want to teach my son a lesson."

Gary: "So the why of your spanking is to teach your toddler a lesson?"

Mother: "Yes."

Gary: "Is there another way that you can teach the same lesson without spanking?"

Mother: (Long pause) "I imagine there are many ways. But I never consider other methods because this worked for my other children."

This was not an unloving mom because she spanked, but she was frustrated because she was fixed on this single method and thought it was the only form of discipline available to adjust her child's misbehavior. She placed a greater value on the *how* of resolving the problem at the expense of the truly greater value, *why*. Why do you want to change this behavior? The *why* behind your thinking is what energizes you to do what you do. Thus, when you lose sight of *why*, *how* actually becomes burdensome.

When we do this in parenting and management, we lock out of our thinking many other good options that might, in fact, be better and far more effective solutions than what we are currently using. Like the copy machine example given earlier, fixing the spanking problem became a greater value than her original *why* behind correcting her child—to teach a moral lesson. There are many ways to teach these lessons. She could have tried loss of privileges, isolation, sit time, natural consequences, encouragement, substitution, and many more positive tactics.

The Rationals know that the *how* of a problem is simply the servant of *why*. To get stuck on *how* is to miss the greater value of *why*. Upon examining *why*, this mom would observe at least half a dozen other "how-to" possibilities. A reasonable *how* for resolving these issues becomes clearer in light of this larger view—a view of the forest, not the trees.

Thinking for a Change

There is a simple, workable, and highly effective means by which you as a mom or dad can make decisions that are right for your children of all ages, without the nagging feeling that you are doing something wrong just because you might be doing something different than your neighbor. The Rational mother sang it, the parrot repeated it, the old gray owl knew of it, and the Howto mother learned it. It is expressed in the following formula.

$$B + g = W + H = (S)\text{olutions that satisfy (N)eeds}$$

Does this equation look confusing? Does it remind you of a bad Algebra 1 experience? Take heart. Actually, it is a rather simple equation/formula, in which you will assign certain values to two letters. The rest of the equation then will become clear and easy to apply. You will assign the value to letters **B** and **g** to produce the meaning of **W**. We can help you with **H**. Put them together, and you will have your solution. Here is the broader meaning of each letter.

B represents your beliefs about the major categories of training. There are seven general categories outlined below that are very much part of your life, and to which only you can assign value. Other areas may be added if you need them.

1. Morality. How do I view right and wrong?

2. Education. How will I educate my child in useful knowledge?

3. Faith and Religion. How strong is my faith, and what do I believe about God?

4. Family/Parenting. What is my parenting style? (This could be mother led, father led, a co-regent leadership, or child led.)

5. Friendships. What is our family's basis for community and friendships?

6. Finances. What are our core values governing earnings, spending and savings?

7. Children. What do I believe about the nature of children, their needs, abilities, and capacities?

8. Other. Add any other values of your own.

In the preceding equation, **g** represents your goals in parenting. The lower case **g** is not a typographical error. While beliefs may not always translate into goals, goals cannot exist without beliefs. Goals must have a reason to exist. They are predicated on our beliefs. Whether you have one child or a dozen children, formulating and articulating a set of family and parenting goals is essential to knowing where you are going with this child. Where do you want to be next week, next month, next year, or in three years with your toddler?

W is the combination of your personal beliefs (**B**) and goals (**g**). Together they form the reasons you do what you do, the all-important *Why*. *Why* you parent the way you parent is based on the values you believe are important, and what you have determined to be worthy and timely goals for your children. *Why* represents the constant beliefs in your hierarchy of values.

H represents *how*, and addresses the methods by which issues, needs, or problems may be addressed. *How* looks at the many options available to solve a particular need in your child's life. It could be a physical, educational, emotional, moral, or corrective need. *How* represents the various methods used to solve a problem or meet a need. *How* represents the variables of application.

With our short glossary of terms we can now venture into a deeper probe of this life and parenting formula. We will start with the need or problem and work backward. There is a need (**N**) or a problem calling for a solution (**S**) or a decision.

Without any further explanation we can summarize the purpose of this chapter in a sentence. Take whatever you believe about life and turn these values into goals. Let the goals determine your training priorities, and use methods that facilitate your goals while meeting your child's needs. If this all makes sense, feel free to turn to the next chapter. But if you desire a more detailed explanation of how to make this equation work for you, continue reading.

Starting with a question

What behavior are you trying to fix? What decision must be made on behalf of your child? What need must be satisfied? What problem must be solved? Are you trying to figure out how to best redirect misbehavior, such as preventing peanut-buttery fingers from touching the sliding door, or two siblings quarreling over a toy? Are you contemplating an educational need? Should you put your child in a playgroup? If so, which playgroup will you choose? Should you start preschool, or begin homeschooling? Is it a potty training need? Which method will you use, and when will you start? Whatever question you have, whatever need is present, whatever problem arises, you are obviously looking for a solution (**S**). Where will you find your solution?

Beliefs and goals

In the Land of Good Reason, we meet Rich and Julie, a thirty-something couple with three children under age 6. While Rich counsels other Rationals regarding investments, Julie manages the home-front, bearing constant witness to the family's hierarchy of values. Rich and Julie believe their job includes preparing 3-year-old Caleb for kindergarten.

The goal is noble, shaped by the parameters of the couple's goals and beliefs regarding education. Here is a listing of their parameters. They believe:

1. Education is not all book-learning.
2. Parents must educate a child in life skills, health and safety, and morality.
3. Educating character is as important as educating the mind.
4. Teaching a toddler self-control and how to sit is foundational to a good education.
5. Parents should be more proactive in education, less reactive.
6. Parents are teachers of learning more than facilitators of discovery.
7. Parents are the primary directors of early education.
8. Parents should create structured opportunities to learn.
9. Education for children can be fun, but when it is not, children still must learn.
10. Parents should create an environment that fosters a joy of learning.

11. Children should be educated in useful knowledge.
12. At all costs, learning must be safe and age-appropriate and all goals must be realistic.

Rich and Julie's beliefs (**B**) about education govern their children's educational goals (**g**). What is listed above forms the parameters into which their goals and parenting management will fit. If any belief conflicts with another belief or goal, then confusion, frustration, and disharmony will find a way into their lives.

To follow along with that point, consider this example. If Rich and Julie believe they should create a conflict-free home environment for Caleb, while holding to their educational goals, then they will encounter major confusion. That belief would conflict with the following principles, to name a few:

1. Parents are primary directors of education.
2. Parents should create structured learning opportunities.
3. Educating children can be fun, but even if it is not, children still must learn.
4. Teaching self-control to a toddler is foundational to effective education.

Let's say Julie is directing 3-year-old Caleb to sit with her for a story. Yet Caleb, in that moment, prefers to march to the beat of his own drum, both figuratively and literally. If Julie stays consistent with her educational beliefs, then she will work with Caleb to sit still for a story. If Caleb's happiness reigns supreme in that instant, then Julie's beliefs about education fly the coop.

You cannot hold goals (**g**) that are antagonistic with your beliefs

APPENDIX B

(**B**) in your parenting. This is the apex, the pinpoint, the exact origin of where parenting frustration and confusion begins. You are serving two masters that are antagonistic in function; one must go. Change your beliefs or change your goals. Rich and Julie's success is due in part to their consistency in beliefs and goals. As long as they stay in harmony, the *why* of their parenting keeps them on track in all areas of Caleb's little life.

It also reduces a tremendous amount of parent frustration. Rich and Julie have a road map and know where they are going and as a result, they have the freedom on some days to take a shortcut or a more scenic route to their destination. That sense of freedom is what reduces fear, doubt, and confusion in early parenting.

Traffic Lights and Chalk Lines

Values, arranged pyramid-style by importance, form a network of convictions that both motivates and restrains parents. They may be likened to a traffic signal: red, yellow, and green, controlling what we allow ourselves and our children to do or not to do at different times. These signals do not change our goals, but they govern how our goals are met.

Every mom and dad has a piece of chalk, figuratively speaking, that they use to "draw the line." The self-imposed restrictions derived from our hierarchy of values establish personal lines of demarcation. These are the nonnegotiable reference points that our goals must fit inside—the "DO NOT CROSS" lines. The question each family must decide is, "Where do you draw the line?"

As important as personal goals are, they must have some moral boundaries. The goal of a successful student is noble. But will it be okay to cheat on tests to get ahead? Is that acceptable to you? Most parents would of course say "No!" without hesitation. They would do so because the goal of academic excellence cannot be achieved outside the nonnegotiable moral parameters. Why is this the case? Because you know that competence and character go hand in hand. You do not want to raise a smart child who lacks integrity.

So, how far are you willing to go to make your child happy? Is it okay if he pulls a few toys out of the neighbor's yard and keeps them in his playroom? Where do you draw that line? Your 2-year-old child finds joy in throwing pebbles in the air, but can he throw them at the house next door? Your child's actions must be monitored for moral liability.

Your Family is Unique

Finally, please understand that all family beliefs and goals must be considered within the context of their own uniqueness. The uniqueness of your family is what creates the variables in parenting. Does Dad work a swing shift? Does Mom work outside the home? Do you use a nanny or have a live-in mother-in-law? Is Mom on call every third weekend? Does Dad work at home or travel for business? Are you parenting your first toddler or your seventh? How many older siblings are doting over your toddler's cuteness? Is your child in daycare or preschool? Are you parenting without a spouse around?

The point is that all families have a different set of circumstances, continually changing and evolving, that influences the way we parent. Families also have different sets of beliefs. Some families let their children watch anything the T.V. offers, while others do not allow their children to watch television at all. Some parents enjoy Santa

Claus in the Christmas scene, and some do not celebrate Christmas. The unique differences do not necessarily mean that some families are wrong.

Therefore, solving parenting issues cannot come out of a canned, one-size-fits-all program. You must forge your own answers for the benefit of your family. Your home is not like your neighbor's home. Your lifestyle is different than your sister's. Your beliefs may be in conflict with those of your parents. Your standards may be different, either higher or lower than your friends. Every home has a set of variables influencing the way a child is raised, and your family is no different.

Summary

To make confident decisions in parenting you need to know:

1. What are your beliefs about the general categories of parenting?
2. What are your goals for parenting?
3. How will you satisfy the why of your beliefs?

The formula, **B + g = W + H = Solutions**, will guide you to your answers. You will be better equipped to solve toddler moments of crisis when you know what you believe, why you believe it, and how you will execute these values. It will get you to your destination without you second-guessing whether your child was somehow emotionally or intellectually short-changed for life. Applied daily, it will keep you in harmony with your beliefs and free from doubts. Enjoy the gentle breeze, and do not lose sight of the *why* behind the *how*.

Index

Alphabet Training 123
Attention Span 119

Bath Time 103
Bedtime 103
Bedtime Routine 105
Beliefs, Establishing 230
Beliefs and Goals 232
Boundaries
    Emotional 41
    Self-Control 41

Children and Books 213
Collateral Value and Moral Training 32
Choices, Problem with 69, 72
    Addiction 75
    Moral Choices 67
    Non-moral Choices 67
Chores 181
Community, Importance of 198
Community Values 52
Conscience
    Defending/Accusing Mechanism 55
    Activities of the Conscience 53
    Healthy Conscience 58
    Higher Conscience 51
    Lower Conscience 52
    Moral Search Mechanism 56
    Moral Warehouse 53
    Prohibitive Conscience 59
    Prohibitive Conscience Test 60

Prompting/Confirming Mechanism 54
Positive Conscience 58
Unhealthy Conscience 58
Working of 47-48, 51
Consequences
Isolation 167
Natural 165
Logical 166
Correction, Laws of 153
Correction Defined 155
Correction Topics
Apologies vs. Seeking Forgiveness 161
Childishness and Defiance 156
Promoting Learning 158
The Role of Punishment .160
Couch Time 102
Curiosity 13

Developmental Placement and Leaning Difficulties 140
Placement Factors 143
Emotional Challenges .145
Later Birthdays 143
Premature Birth 144
Slower Development .145
Social Challenges 145
School Stressfulness 141
Testing 145
When of Placement 142
Why needed 138
Developmental Concepts of Capacity and Desire 154
Moral Readiness 154

Educational Choices 148
Emotional Intelligence 39

Encouragement, Tools of 182-187
Extremism defined 43

Factors of Learning 29, 115
Fears, Understanding Childhood 193-198
Fence, Concept of 86-87
        What and Where 94
Freedoms
        Decision-Making 72
        Physical 75
        Verbal 75
Free Playtime 97
Focusing Skills 119
Formula of Reason 229
Forgiveness, power of 164
Funnel, Analogy 69

Gender Differences 25
Goals, Setting 88, 224

Happiness Quotient 42
Heart of the Child 46
How/Why Dichotomy 223, 225

Imagination 14
        Imagination and play 15
Immediate Gratification 38
Instruction, Pre-activity 179
Intelligence Quotient 39
Interrupt Courtesy 36

Kindergarten preparation 113

Land of Good Reason 219

Leaning and
      Chaos 30
      Intellectual 32
      Moral 32
      Skills 31, 118

Marshmallow Test 40
Mealtime 106
Mealtime Guidelines 107
Mealtime Manners .187-193
Moral Boundaries .24, 234
Moral Training and Collateral Value 32

Naptime Transitions 100

Parenting
      Outside the Funnel 69
Physical Freedoms 75
Play and
      Benefits of 17
      Construction 18
      Diagram 16
      Educational Value 18
      Imagination 15
      Leaning Opportunities 17
      Limits of Play .22-26
      Moral Value 21
      Therapeutic value 18
Play and Limits
      Developmental 22
      Emotional 23
      Gender 25
      Intellectual 24
      Moral 24

Playtime with Friends 98
Playtime, Types of 97-98
    Independent 120
    Play Dates 133
Positive Speech 178
Proactive Teaching Style 116
Puzzles 122

Rest-time 100
Roomtime 96
Routine, Times of
    Afternoon 99
    Evening 101
    Morning 94
Routine
    Bedtime 105
    Looks like 87
    Value of 86
    Writing Out 91

School Readiness and
    Art 125
    Attention Span 119
    Focusing Skills 120
    History 127
    Math 123
    Mom 132
    Music 126
    Penmanship 124
    Reading 121
    Science 128
    Social Interaction 132
    Teachers 129

Self-Control
    Testing 39-41
    Training 38, 174
Sleep, Importance of 114
    Optimal Alertness 115
    Passive Chronic Fatigue .115
    Sleep Ranges 114
Structuring Your Child's Day 83, 117
Structured Play Time 97
Successful Education Basics .148

Trial-and-Error Teaching Style 116
Toys
    Games, Types of 207
    Games, Traditional 208
    Gender Toys 206
    Guidelines for Choosing 204
    Tidying Up Toys 215
    When Too Many 214

Verbal Freedoms 75-77
Video Time 98

Whining 181
What and Where, Concept of 94
Whole Child 33-35
Wise in His Own Eyes 67